D1202473

"This book will be helpful for anyone interested
and active in working on community issues."

— *Martin Adams, Office of the Mayor,*
City of Minneapolis

✳

"Mayer's conclusions about what it takes
to build community capacity can
guide all who are committed to
making their communities better places."

— *Terri Barreiro, Vice President*
United Way of Minneapolis Area

✳

"No matter the size of the foundation or
the community, this book can help you revisit your
mission, strengthen your strategic plan,
and serve your community more thoughtfully."

— *Ruth Heffron, Executive Director,*
Trident Community Foundation,
Charleston, South Carolina

Building Community Capacity:
The Potential *of* Community Foundations

Steven E. Mayer

Rainbow Research, Inc.
Minneapolis

This book is available at a special discount when
ordered in quantities. For information, contact

Publications Department
Rainbow Research, Inc.
621 West Lake Street
Minneapolis, MN 55408

Published by:
Rainbow Research, Inc.
621 West Lake Street
Minneapolis, MN 55408

ISBN 0-9624428-4-4
First Edition, First Printing
Printed in the United States of America

 This book, not including the cover, contains:
50% pre-consumer
0% post-consumer

NWST
AEM 8907

Table of Contents

Continued

Table of Contents, *continued*

Table of Contents, *continued*

Foreword

A strong national network of community foundations is good for communities. It is also good for the national philanthropies that aim to have an effective connection to those communities. The Ford Foundation developed the Leadership Program for Community Foundations with several thoughts in mind. Besides the inherent value of strengthening local capacity, the benefits to Ford of working with community foundations were obvious to the architects of the program.

Community foundations can be a constant source of good new ideas, local expertise, and financial support for local programs that would be hard pressed to get support from a national foundation like Ford. It's a lot easier for us to spend resources effectively in a city or region if the community foundation has convened the relevant and often diverse constituencies, and found the common ground necessary to move forward. This helps develop local leadership, reinforces local definition and ownership of the problem, and increases the probability that future philanthropic dollars will be spent effectively.

The Leadership Program was launched in 1987, when fewer than 25 of the over 300 existing community foundations had assets over $25 million. The particular niche that Ford chose to fill in the limited array of capacity-building efforts aimed at community foundations was one of accelerating the growth and community leadership of foundations that are small but firmly established. It seemed to us that small community foundations have several clear needs. First, and most simply, they need additional assets to establish a level of credibility and stability that helps them become a significant community force. Secondly, they need flexible capacity to enable them to respond most effectively to local needs as they change over time. Finally, small community foundations frequently have limited experience in proactive grantmaking and in taking on active community problem-solving roles. This is largely a luxury associated with bigger community foundations that have both the resources and the staff to take on such activities.

After one round of the Leadership Program, Ford was joined by the John D. and Catherine T. MacArthur Foundation as a substantial partner. The enhanced resources available to the program as a consequence allowed for an increase in the number of participants in the second round as well as a limited number of smaller developmental grants for some of those applicants not selected as finalists. The third and final round of the Leadership Program was funded in 1991.

The Leadership Program was structured to address the needs of community foundations by helping them secure new unrestricted funds, while providing support for the development and implementation of a five-year grants program targeting an important community problem. The goal is to leave the participating community foundation with increased assets for flexible grantmaking as well as enhanced board and staff capacity and commitment to assuming a leadership role in community problem solving.

A central feature of the Leadership Program was the technical assistance and support provided by the project director for the Program at Community Resource Exchange. Because community foundations are by definition isolated from each other geographically, the project director developed a number of mechanisms to encourage cross-site learning and support. The underlying philosophy was one which conveyed to the participants the notion that the Program would be implemented in as flexible and responsive a way as possible to maximize each foundation's growth and enhanced capacity. The project director visited the participating foundations on a regular basis, convened each Round at least annually, subsidized their travel to professional meetings, and brokered specialized technical assistance as needed. The relationships formed among participating community foundation board members, executives, and staff turned out to be an important ingredient in their development.

Another important goal of the Leadership Program was to increase the body of knowledge available to the entire field of community foundations and philanthropy on successful strategies of community foundation development. The empirical literature on this subject was so thin and the participants young enough and diverse enough that it was important to structure a way to document and learn as much as possible from their experience, individually and as a group. We are indebted to Steven Mayer and his colleagues at Rainbow Research for their considerable contribution to this learning enterprise. Rainbow Research encouraged the participating community foundations to be reflective about their development in a way that was helpful to them and contributed to the larger body of knowledge about capacity-building strategies. It developed several important tools for self-evaluation and for assessing benchmarks of progress that will now be available to the larger field. We hope that this volume will fill in some gaps in the literature and prove to be a useful stimulus for continued discussion in the field on the dynamics and strategies of successful community foundation growth and leadership.

Prudence Brown	*Emmett Carson*	*Barrie Pribyl*
Formerly: Ford Foundation	Program Officer	Project Director
Currently: Research Fellow	Governance and	Leadership Program for
Chapin Hall Center	Public Policy	Community Foundations
for Children at the	Ford Foundation	Community Resource
University of Chicago		Exchange

Preface

Many of us today lament that community capacity — that mix of commitment, resources, and skills available to a community to increase its visibility and vitality — is in short supply. There are many reasons for this, ranging from federal budget shifts of the 1980s to globalization of marketplaces, institutional racism, economic dislocations and "compassion fatigue."

But another reason, of immediate concern to readers of this book, is that there is little concerted, intentional effort to *develop* community capacity. The approach that could encourage more investment in community capacity is still submerged by the dominant view that advances "professionalized social service delivery systems" and "charity." The dominant view regrettably emphasizes the needs and deficiencies of people and communities, rather than their strengths and capacities. By fixing individuals, this dominant view assumes, the vitality of community life will be enhanced. We believe that community vitality requires more than an investment in the development of individuals.

We believe community vitality requires an investment in the growing capacity of community groups and institutions that can contribute to community life. One reason for this book, then, is to advance the concept of "community capacity" and how it is generated and deployed.

A second reason for this book is to describe the strategic role that community foundations can play in helping communities build capacity. Said to be the fastest growing segment in philanthropy, there are now more than four hundred community foundations nationally. Probably hundreds of thousands of people have contributed to them or through them.

At Rainbow Research we have paid particular attention to a number of qualities exhibited by community foundations: their mission, the variety of leadership roles they can play, their interactive relationships with different types of agents for healthy communities, and their suitability as a vehicle for "the charitable impulse" (*Joseph, 1989a*). Perhaps most important, a growing number of them are actively learning the strategies of community capacity building.

The Ford Foundation — which underwrote the research leading to this book — has long been interested in the potential of community foundations. While not the first large national funder to recognize the potential of community foundations, it became persuaded that community foundations could do what Ford itself could not do — act locally.

The Ford Foundation saw the potential of community foundations as generators of local philanthropic capital and local leadership in resolving modern urban, rural, and regional problems. It developed the Leadership Program for Community Foundations specifically to build on that potential. This five-year Program has been so successful in inducing growth and usefulness among the participating community foundations that the Program itself offers excellent instruction to others willing to invest in community capacity.

The third reason this book is being written, then, is to provide readers with an understanding of the features of a growth-inducing program of support. While the details pertain to a large foundation's grantmaking program we believe they define the very essence of "support," and are applicable more widely.

Our job at Rainbow Research, once the Leadership Program began, was to increase the body of knowledge available to the larger world of philanthropy, national nonprofit and local community groups, and other public and private partners about successful strategies and development for building organizational and community capacity.

To learn how community foundations grow and develop to become increasingly useful institutions serving their communities we visited 18 of the 27 community foundations participating in the Leadership Program in their first, second, and fifth years of participation. We reviewed their public and private reports, listened to them at the annual meetings of Program participants, interviewed them at their national meetings, conversed by phone, and conducted annual surveys.

As the participants' understanding of the potential of community foundations grew, so did ours. We became aware that we were seeing the emergence of a new form of community foundation, one that could truly become more useful to its community. This new form seriously studied and valued the role of "catalyst" — making something happen by mobilizing commitment, by smart allocation of small amounts of philanthropic capital, and by encouraging community building skills in a variety of other community groups.

In writing this book I'm indebted to the vision and support of Prudence Brown. As the principal program officer at the Ford Foundation during the design and implementation of this Program, Prue clearly incorporated those rare qualities of focus, simplicity, and drive into the very fiber of this Program. The Leadership Program is probably the best designed and most productive program I've examined in 20 years of practice. Participants benefited from the unusually high-quality features designed into the Program. Those not able to participate can learn from their experience through Ford's intention to support knowledge development and knowledge transfer — another purpose of this book. Thanks go also to Emmett Carson who inherited this project in his position as Program Officer in the Governance and Public Policy Division and supported the printing and distribution of this book.

A good design suffers without good implementation. Barrie Pribyl, Project Director for this Leadership Program deserves credit for the success of this endeavor. Housed at the Community Resource Exchange in New York, Barrie was charged with all aspects of implementation, from the application process to annual meetings of participants to technical assistance. Her collegial perspective and support was invaluable to all participants in the Program.

Finally I want to salute the executive directors and board leadership of the participating community foundations. At our first gathering I said my role and theirs was to be "co-discoverers" — that we'd be charting new land and helping each other understand and explain what we found there. Their pioneering spirit was infectious. As individuals they are truly community builders and are helping their institutions grow into this important role as well. This book is dedicated to their work and to the work of countless other women and men who endeavor to strengthen the capacity of their community.

Steven E. Mayer, Ph.D.
Executive Director
Rainbow Research, Inc.

February 28, 1994
Minneapolis

Acknowledgements

A short but sincere thanks to some of the people who contributed to the finished product. To Mary Lilja, of Lilja, Ink, a conscientious editor who encouraged me to keep to the larger context, and to say what I had to say (and no more). To Jerie Heille, of the Amherst H. Wilder Foundation, whose sense of style and attention to design detail gave this book its elegant appearance. To Kristine Scott, computer production coordinator at Rainbow Research, whose mastery of word processing and desktop publishing was the key to our production capability. To Sharon Ramirez, colleague at Rainbow Research, who collected and assembled the numerical data from participating community foundations over the years. And to Jean Hammink, whose steadfast support of me and my work seems to know no bounds.

*Dedicated to
the memory of
M. Dean Havron*

Chapter One

Community Capacity, Community Groups, and Community Foundations

In this chapter, we examine the concept of community capacity: what it means and how it is developed. Then we look at a variety of community institutions — families, neighborhood and community development groups, churches, government, charities and others — and discuss how each builds capacity. Finally, we look at community foundations and explore their growing influence and role as builders of community capacity.

The concept of community capacity

People live in communities. But the real importance of "living in community" is that people — and groups of people — develop the ways and means to care for each other, nurture talents and leadership that enhance the quality of community life, and tackle problems that threaten the community.

When people do these things, communities become healthy; when they do not, communities deteriorate. Communities that have the ways and means to undertake challenges exhibit "capacity."

Without capacity, communities are merely collections of individuals acting without concern for the common good, and are without the necessary ingredients required to develop a healthier community. Communities without capacity are not communities in any meaningful sense, but have given way to apathy, poverty, and ineptitude.

So what is community capacity? We suggest the following definition:

> **Community capacity is the combined influence of a community's commitment, resources, and skills which can be deployed to build on community strengths and address community problems.**

Clarification of some terms used in this definition may be helpful.

Commitment refers to a community-held will to act based on awareness of problems, opportunities, and workable solutions. It refers also to a heightened state of support in key sectors of the community to address problems, solve problems, and strengthen community responses.

Resources refers to financial assets and the means to deploy them intelligently and fairly. It also includes information or guidelines that ensure the best use of funds.

Skills includes all the talents and expertise of individuals and organizations that can be marshaled to address problems, seize opportunities, and add strength to existing and emerging institutions.

Communities and the groups and institutions within them vary tremendously in capacity. Capacity is gained in degrees, sometimes slowly, other times rapidly. All communities and community groups, even those most seemingly broken down, have capacity in some measure and, we believe, are capable of developing more. They can increase their ability to build community, to grow with opportunities, and to confront threats to the community's health and viability.

How capacity is developed

The three essential ingredients of community capacity — commitment, resources, and skills — don't "just happen." Rather, they are developed through effort and will, initiative and leadership.

For example, effort, will, initiative, and leadership are needed to:

- educate community members, help shape opinion, and galvanize commitment to act.

- attract and collect financial resources, compile information, and shape ways for deploying these resources to "catalyze" change in the way problems are addressed and opportunities for growth seized.

- organize people and work, develop skills, and coordinate or manage a sustained effort that builds up the positive qualities of community life that begin to resolve a problem.

The challenge for a community group or institution struggling to gain more capacity is to develop its own commitment, resources, and skills. The challenge for those outside that particular group but wishing to help is to create opportunities appropriate for that group that can help it grow in capacity.

Barriers can sometimes limit the growth of capacity. Sometimes these barriers are maintained by malevolent or ignorant forces; other times they are maintained by habit or lack of vision or leadership. Sometimes the right opportunities to develop capacity have not come along or been recognized as opportunities. These barriers, however, can be overcome.

Communities and the groups and institutions within them can be intentional and strategic in their desire to develop capacity. Capacity growth in a community group can be stimulated by other groups or institutions outside it. In other words, communities can attract investment from outside in ways that stimulate their capacity development. Once a group has developed some measure of capacity, it can help to stimulate capacity development in others.

All kinds of community groups contribute to community capacity to some degree. They contribute first by developing their own capacity, and then by encouraging the development of capacity in others.

For example, when a community foundation — a relatively recent arrival on the community building scene — grows in its capacity, it can contribute to capacity development in other community groups and institutions. Today, most community foundations are still in the process of developing their own capacity, but many have learned to deploy it successfully in the service of building capacity in other arenas of community life. The potential of community foundations for adding to community capacity — to the capacity of families, neighborhood and community development, associations and coalitions, charities, schools, churches and other religious institutions, government, small and large businesses and even other foundations — is substantial.

As with other community groups, the development of capacity within a community foundation does not "just happen." It happens when the community foundation decides to develop capacity — to build commitment, mobilize resources, and develop skills. These events can be induced, even put on a "fast track," by stimulation from outside.

A preview of this book

Most of this book is devoted to describing a program that successfully stimulated growth in a select group of community foundations. It tracks the growth of these community foundations, how they developed their capacity, and how they have helped create capacity in their communities.

Before we examine this program, however, we will examine a variety of other community organizations and how they contribute to building community capacity. This context is important — we have learned that community foundations do not work in isolation to achieve their goals, but *with and through* these other groups.

Chapter Two describes this program, the Leadership Program for Community Foundations.

Chapters Three, Four, and Five describe how community foundations participating in the Program developed their capacities: their financial resource development capacities, their organization building and administrative capacities, and their community leadership capacities. Chapter Six describes the results of their efforts to stimulate capacity growth in others through their "community leadership initiatives."

Chapter Seven summarizes participants' accomplishments and evaluates the features of the Leadership Program that contributed to their success — so that other community groups and institutions can design similar, capacity-engendering programs for themselves.

Contributions of different community institutions to community capacity

It is important to understand how a variety of community groups and institutions contribute to community capacity, because each kind is a potential partner with community foundations in their shared work of strengthening the viability and vitality of communities. In their partnership, both can gain in capacity, as is revealed in later chapters.

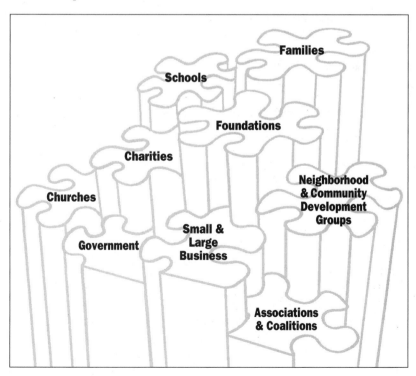

Families

Families, in their informal way, have been the first agent of community capacity building since the beginning of recorded history.

Commitment. Families help generate and preserve value systems *(Gardner, 1991)*. Nature appears to assign to families the task of easing individuals into the larger community and of imparting the rules and norms of behavior. Families are designed to nurture, encourage, and support their members as their participation in the larger community increases.

Resources. Families consume goods and services, and they also produce them. They spend money and save it. Families accumulate material resources, and in doing so, demonstrate to their children necessary values and skills.

Skills. In both subtle and overt ways, families learn, encourage learning, and in essence, teach the principles of capacity building. They show their members the uses of information, material resources, and the values that underlie their acquisition and deployment. Families teach — in varying degrees — problem solving, planning, organizational development, and management.

Neighborhood and community development groups

Neighborhoods, for the past several decades, have been the next geographically defined element of community, at least for urban and perhaps suburban Americans. They reveal and represent much of the world to those who reside there. They symbolize safety or danger. They provide the place for friendly gatherings or isolating alienation. Neighborhood groups mobilize (or don't) to preserve or secure a better quality of life for their residents.

Neighborhoods and clusters of neighborhoods embrace countless groups that operate without regard to official or institutional structures *(Kretzmann and McKnight, 1993)*. Many of these are clubs or associations of persons gathering for some common purpose.

They meet periodically and support themselves. These include block clubs, garden clubs, service clubs, book clubs, ethnic affinity clubs, and more. Others are structured "neighborhood associations," groups of people that identify with neighborhood-related causes and issues. Neighborhood-based organizations have flourished in the last ten years, partly because of the decentralization of financial resources and partly because of a rediscovery of the "grassroots" as a political bedrock.

Commitment. Neighborhood and development groups create support for change, as well as for stability. They support political movements behind better housing, schools, recreation, health, safety, and other issues. In addition, neighborhoods or clusters of neighborhoods create processes for facilitating governance and justice, such as elections, juries, political parties, police, and advocacy groups.

Resources. Neighborhoods are host to retail and service areas, to formal institutions for spending, saving, and investing. Considerable money changes hands in neighborhoods. Most of the formal institutions that exist in neighborhoods, like schools, parks, churches and other religious institutions, draw their support from a larger territory — several neighborhoods together, or urban districts made up of several neighborhoods and beyond.

Skills. Though largely informal, skills provide an important fabric to community life and allow individuals to "live in community." They provide capacity for the larger community because, by definition, they are organized around common issues, themes or interests. Individuals educate each other and the larger community, raise money in support of projects they want to promote, and develop the political and organizational skills to accomplish their goals.

Associations and coalitions

In unity there is strength and, recognizing this, voluntary groups and nonprofit organizations have joined together at various levels to gain greater voice and influence in decision-making arenas that affect them.

Commitment. Associations and coalitions by definition represent the mutual commitment of their members to their common purpose. People organize geographically as well as by issue area or interests. At the neighborhood level, individuals coalesce and form a neighborhood group. At the city level, neighborhood groups become the city's Neighborhood Resource Center. At the national level, they become the National Association of Neighborhoods. Coalescing occurs along issue areas or occupational lines. The National Coalition Against Domestic Violence has a membership of statewide coalitions. The National Association of Social Workers has state chapters of individuals.

Resources. Membership organizations usually measure their assets in membership, not dollars. Larger organizations have more clout with those they're trying to influence — typically legislative or regulatory bodies, groups that affect the rules and regulations affecting their particular arena and occupation.

Skills. A common purpose of associations and coalitions is to enhance their members' skills. They do this through a variety of "member services" such as specialized publications, training programs, and annual conferences. The more sophisticated also have programs of "mentoring" or "technical assistance" to help member individuals or organizations develop their administrative, programming, or leadership skills.

Charities

Charities provide relief to individuals suffering from economic disaster (unemployment or dislocation), natural disaster (floods, illness, cultural deprivation), or family disaster (abuse or neglect).

Commitment. Charitable organizations reflect society's commitment to help those who are suffering. They create a culture of concern and caring. Charitable organizations appeal to individuals who share that concern, recruiting them to help. These community institutions have their roots in the Judeo-Christian imperative of caring for those in need; "caring" and "charity" come from the same Latin root, "caritas."

Resources. Charities raise money from the general public, seeking donations from individuals, from businesses and corporations, from organized philanthropies, and religious institutions. In the 20th Century, charities in this country have become secularized. As so-called "public charities," they are recognized by the Internal Revenue Service for serving a public good and are exempted from paying corporate income tax. Almost all public charities have developed fairly sophisticated administrative structures and funding mechanisms.

Skills. In recent decades, at the insistence of supporters, charities became more efficient, borrowing heavily from the techniques of the manufacturing sector and from post-industrial management science. Charitable concern and caring is now institutionalized in the form of nonprofit, tax-exempt "service delivery programs," requiring skilled managers.

Schools

In today's society, schools are major agents of skills and values learning by children and youth. Education is largely a public function supported by local government.

Commitment. Schools reflect the commitment of society to educate the young, and to prepare young people for adult life. What
"adult life" means, and what preparation for it is valid, has been
the subject of interesting debates in the past two decades. Different parties to these debates wish to commit schools to training our
young people for vocational, family, organizational, or community
life. Different school systems and curricula reflect these differences
in priorities.

Resources. The commitment to public education is substantial; its
line in public budgets, especially at the state and county levels, is
typically among the largest of all public expenditures.

Skills. Public schools are charged with teaching their students the
skills required to play a constructive role in society. How successful they are varies, of course, from school district to school district,
depending considerably on the commitment and resources deployed to further this goal.

Churches and other religious institutions

Religious institutions, particularly places of worship, grew out of
the natural wish of persons for a place for spiritual communion
with a higher power and with each other.

Commitment. While most religious institutions exist for the spiritual and moral development of their congregation, many conduct
charitable activities such as soup kitchens, clothes closets, or outreach to isolated people. An increasing number are undertaking or
participating as partners in projects such as Habitat for Humanity
and other housing or economic development activities.

Resources. Religious congregations have people power. Like neighborhoods (which historically grew up around churches), they have
the capacity to mobilize and involve people in issues. They also collect "offerings" or charge dues, a portion of which can be used for
charitable or development projects. At the diocesan level and higher,

there frequently are considerable financial resources in the form of endowments, pension funds, and real estate.

Skills. The skills of religious congregations are largely the skills of their individual members, plus the leadership. When church members decide to do something — and this can be said of most community groups — the skills and resources are typically found, often from within.

Government

Government at all levels — national, state, and local — plays a role in the development of community capacity.

Commitment. Government reflects the will of the people through a representational process in which all citizens can participate. "Will" gets reinterpreted as it proceeds up the legislative and policy making ladders and then down through the bureaucratic and regulatory ladders, through the process we call "politics." It includes ongoing debate about the limits of public responsibility. For example, is it government's responsibility to provide mental health services or is it the individual's or family's concern? If the government is responsible, what level is appropriate — local, state, or federal? If it's not the government's responsibility, is it the private sector's or the independent sector's responsibility?

Resources. However the debate rages, public sector budgets in the 1990s tend to be fairly large — even gigantic — relative to private and independent sector budgets, though this varies by jurisdiction. Federal, state, municipalities, and special districts (parks, schools) have the power to tax and to issue bonds. How they exercise that power is highly politicized, as is the way budgets are created.

Skills. The process of politics encourages public education and issue awareness efforts, meetings that seek consensus on priorities, and coalition building — all key ingredients of community capacity building.

13

Small and large businesses

The private or commercial sector exists primarily to create private capacity, not community capacity. Since community vitality often depends on the vitality of the community's business sector there is a close, but complex, connection. By producing goods and services, businesses affect community capacity in a number of ways.

Commitment. In most communities, business leaders have helped to organize constructive responses to stresses that affect community life. From service clubs to recreational and cultural facilities to civic improvement projects, the business sector demonstrates the role it can play in making communities more livable. Business leadership is frequently credited with helping to meet the campaign goals of United Way and other public charities that respond to human needs.

Resources. Work creates wealth and other resources. Businesses provide the tax base used by the public sector, by creating jobs and building facilities that add value to owned property. Individuals with steady employment in positions that pay decently can share in that wealth, allowing them more choices in education, health, recreation, and material pursuits, as well as allowing more time to participate in community activities.

Skills. Many of the skills developed for use on the job, whether manual or administrative, can also be used outside of formal employment in community building activities.

Foundations

Most communities have at least one foundation with the commitment and financial resources dedicated to serving some aspect of community life. The Foundation Center *(1992)*, a national information clearinghouse, lists 8,729 foundations throughout the United States, with concentrations in the major population centers, particularly where wealth is "old" rather than "new." The purposes of foundations vary widely, though all have been judged by the Internal Revenue Service to be serving a public interest.

Commitment. The extent to which foundations are committed to building community capacity varies widely. Some act from the charitable model in which the foundation's resources are directed to the relief of suffering in one or more of its various forms. Others are committed to the development model in which the foundation's resources are directed to the development of some aspect of community capacity. One can detect in their brochures and reports considerable confusion about these two different models and inconsistent practices; this is largely because the development model is still quite new and its principles are emerging.

Resources. The 1992 Foundation Directory reports that the 8,729 foundations control more than $134 billion in assets. This varies considerably among the four types of foundations: independent foundations, community foundations, company-sponsored foundations, and operating foundations.

So-called independent foundations are by far the largest in number (7,277) and in assets ($115 billion). The capital generally derives from a single source, such as an individual, a family, or group of individuals, and decisions are made by the donor's family, its representatives, or an independent board of directors. While the financial resources of foundations are substantial, they are small in comparison to public budgets that exist in the same regions. Even the poorest counties in the country have budgets that address human issues (through both the charitable and development modes) far in excess of the monies available from institutional philanthropy.

Skills. When foundation trustees meet to decide how to distribute the year's allocation of grantmaking dollars, it is typically in private. Their decisions are informed by a process that may not involve public input, citizen participation, or community involvement.

Some foundations, however, want to operate in a style that is more inclusive of community input and more directed to enhancing community capacity. How much they do this depends on a number of factors, including their type. Community foundations, for example, increasingly have "advisory committees" made up of individuals connected to community groups who are knowledgeable about community issues. With company-sponsored foundations, decision-making is increasingly advised by committees of employees — a workplace-defined community.

Operating foundations do not give grants, but operate programs themselves — typically research, public education, social service, and community development — and vary as to how much they contribute to gains in community commitment, resources, and skills.

Independent foundations, the largest in number, probably vary the most in how they operate. A small but growing number seek community involvement in the design of programs. Another group, also small but growing, is striving to embrace the development model and keep it distinct from the charity model, intending to expand the capacity of community groups and community building mechanisms to become increasingly productive.

Capacity and the interconnection of community groups

A community group or institution — whether a family, neighborhood group, charity, school, or foundation — gets its capacity from drawing on the commitment, resources, and skills from those within and around it. A group or institution must first develop capacity in and for itself before it can help develop capacity in others.

If parents do not have commitment, resources, and skills in their role as parents, they will have little to impart to their children. The adult(s) in the family has to be ahead of the children in capacity development if the children are to grow.

If local businesses have little capacity, they can offer little to potential employees in productive work, to current employees in opportunities to develop their skills, and to the community in payroll and taxes.

If neighborhood or development groups can't mobilize people, gather resources, and help people learn to work productively, few people and neighborhoods will benefit.

If schools cannot develop a commitment in their students or their students' parents, if they cannot gather the resources required to help students learn productively, and if they cannot induce skills in students, then few students and their present and future families will benefit.

If foundations cannot decide what aspects of community life to support, if they cannot build up their financial resources and allocate them astutely in the service of capacity building, and if they cannot stimulate the growth of community building skills in individuals and institutions, then community life will not directly benefit.

The task of taking on capacity is one of drawing on the commitment, resources, and skills extended by others, and building up one's own group to become stronger and healthier.

It is clear that some community institutions are better adapted or suited to creating capacity than others. Some take on considerably more capacity than they help create elsewhere, whereas others may be highly efficient, creating as much or more capacity in others as in themselves.

As observed in the last ten years, community foundations are ideally suited for capacity building work — both creating it for themselves and helping to create it elsewhere in the community. Not all community foundations intentionally build capacity elsewhere; most are still more adept at fueling their own institutional development than in helping others create it. Not all community foundations are designed to or intend to create capacity in others, and not all succeed.

Several basic characteristics of community foundations make them ideally suited to the business of creating community capacity. In the next section, the history, structure, and purposes of community foundations are examined.

Community foundations

Community foundations differ significantly from other kinds of foundations. Financial resources for a community foundation come from multiple sources — from individuals living in the community, as well as from a variety of local public and private institutions, including government and foundations. Their interests and efforts are limited to a particular region and typically for the intended benefit of that region. Decisions made by directors are meant to represent the diverse interest in the community.

Community foundation definitions and missions

What exactly is a community foundation? This is a question which even the industry has a difficult time answering with clarity and brevity.

The Council on Foundations, the national industry membership association which includes private, corporate, and community foundations, took months in committee to agree on a definition. The definition eventually approved by the Council on Foundations (1992(a)) is:

A community foundation is a tax-exempt, not-for-profit, autonomous, publicly-supported, philanthropic institution organized and operated primarily as a permanent collection of endowed funds for the long-term benefit of a defined geographic area.

Each community foundation: • is officially recognized by the Internal Revenue Service as tax-exempt under Section 501(c)(3); • meets the public support test under Section 170(b)I(A)(vi) as modified by Treas. Reg. 1.170A- 9(e)(10); • has a governing body broadly representative of the general public; • operates primarily as a grantmaking institution and may also provide direct charitable services; • focuses its primary grantmaking and charitable services within a defined geographic area no larger than three states.

Additional perspectives can be gleaned from major spokespeople for the field. A few samples:

"A community foundation is an organization to which persons or entities of any kind can give funds of almost any kind to meet the perceived needs of a community in any charitable field." *(Struckhoff, 1991).*

"Community foundations provide organized, professional philanthropy without losing the qualities of humanness, spontaneity and flexibility. [They] serve as a meeting ground for collaboration with both individual and institutional grantmakers. [They] can bring those seeking to acquire power into the same room with those seeking to maintain power. [They] permit donors to contribute today where proceeds can be used by future generations." *(Joseph, 1990).*

"Community foundations exercise leadership as conveners around community needs, through asset growth, by helping nonprofit organizations, and through catalytic leadership in dealing with critical issues." *(Magat, 1989).*

At the risk of reducing these descriptions and definitions to a level that has little meaning at all, consider three key underlying themes. A community foundation is:

- a local, geographically defined, community-based organization;

- a collection of charitable funds collected under the rules of the IRS governing charitable organizations and managed for the benefit of the community;

- an organization focused on service to different sectors of the community — to individual donors, to charitable organizations, and to the community at large.

Distribution, size, and growth of community foundations

While the essence of community foundations may be difficult to express, what is indisputable is their growing popularity, size, and influence. Some indicators reflecting their size and activity nationally:

Their number. There are 411 known community foundations in the United States *(Foundation Center, 1991)*. Community foundations exist all over the country, but they are concentrated in number and size in the major population centers and areas of wealth, especially older ones. The 50 wealthiest are shown on an adjoining map. For an illuminating presentation of the early history of community foundations, see Newman, (1989).

Financial assets. Collectively, the assets of community foundations exceed $8 billion *(Columbus Foundation, 1992)*. Most of these assets are controlled by a few community foundations. One-third of them hold about 97 percent of the assets *(Columbus Foundation, 1992)*. Most are small, financially speaking; two-thirds have assets of less than $10 million *(Council on Foundations, 1991)*.

Locations of the 50 largest (in total funds) Community Foundations

Source: Columbus Foundation, 1992

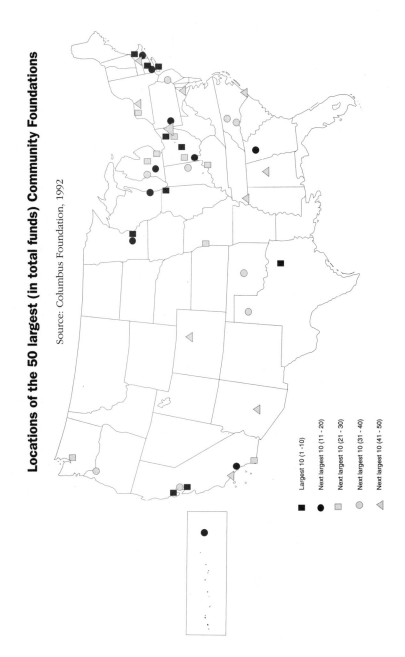

Largest 10 (1 -10) ■

Next largest 10 (11 - 20) ●

Next largest 10 (21 - 30) ▣

Next largest 10 (31 - 40) ●

Next largest 10 (41 - 50) ◀

Growth in assets. Community foundations are said to be the fastest growing segment in organized philanthropy. Over a five-year period, from 1985 to 1990, community foundations grew at a rate of 89 percent, by one estimate *(Council on Foundations, 1992(b))*.

The number reporting to the Foundation Center, which compiles industry statistics, increased by 55 percent during the 1980s *(Foundation Center, 1991)*.

Grantmaking. While the level of assets measures financial size, it says nothing about the usefulness of that money. It is used to make grants, typically to other nonprofit organizations, that meet the guidelines created by the foundation. A total of $376 million was distributed in grants by 187 different community foundations in 1990 *(Council on Foundations, 1991)*.

There is tremendous variation in grantmaking activity. Only 20 community foundations awarded $5 million or more in grants, and together they accounted for nearly two-thirds of all funds distributed by the 282 community foundations the Foundation Center surveyed in 1989.

What do community foundations support through their grantmaking? Just more than half of respondents' grant dollars went to "human services" (27 percent) and "education" (26 percent). The balance went to "public/society benefit" (14 percent), "health" (14 percent), "arts/culture/humanities" (13 percent), "religion" (2 percent), and "other" (5 percent) *(Council on Foundations, 1992(b))*.

Growing role in the community. While their growth in financial assets and in grantmaking is impressive, the real story lies in the growing activity and changing roles of community foundations.

The Council on Foundations points to a level of grantmaking activity among community foundations disproportionate to their size. "While making up less than 1 percent of all U.S. foundations in 1989, community foundations awarded 5.4 percent of all grant dollars, received 10 percent of all new gifts and held 4.4 percent of all foundation assets." *(Council on Foundations, 1992(b))*.

"Community foundations represent a relatively small but extremely vital component of the foundation universe . . . [T]heir leadership role increased along with stepped up demands for private initiatives to solve local problems . . ." *(Foundation Center, 1991)*.

Attendance at the annual Fall Workshop for Community Foundations has risen dramatically over the years. Sessions that are in demand go beyond simple grantmaking and administration; they deal with constructive leadership roles in their communities that help resolve community-wide problems.

Criticisms and challenges from the field

The rapid growth of any kind of institution, especially one that both collects and distributes funds, is likely to invite greater public scrutiny, caveats, and criticism. Concerns can be grouped around the following themes:

Accountability and community leadership. "By intent and definition, a community foundation has no single, fixed, active purpose" *(Hammack, 1989)*. In other words, community foundations are free to seek out the best contemporary uses of philanthropic dollars. This gives community foundations considerable flexibility in the role they play.

Their role warrants scrutiny. Since community foundations are "more public" than private foundations, they face higher standards of accountability, says an industry watchdog group, the National Committee on Responsive Philanthropy (NCRP). Through their growing wealth, community foundations have "increasing power to do good or evil." *(Bothwell, 1989)*.

Bothwell notes that it is the role of citizen activists, as well as foundation activists who want to improve their communities, to assess how well their community foundations are doing and to determine how to redesign inadequate community foundation activities.

Foremost, he says, is public accountability, the formal interaction between foundations and the public. This includes, at a minimum, reporting to the IRS such required information as staff and board descriptions, grant recipients, and amounts awarded. But a community foundation "worthy of the name," according to Bothwell, should voluntarily publish information and hold public meetings to share the foundation's plans and commitments to different program priorities.

A second broad area posed by Bothwell for accountability is "accessibility by all grantseekers." Particularly challenging and important is accessibility to grantseekers who are unknown to staff or board, as a way to broaden the foundation's view.

A third area is "responsiveness." While acknowledging the importance of responsiveness to the donor's wishes and to the governing body's policies and IRS regulations, the area of greatest concern to NCRP is responsiveness in grantmaking. Is a community foundation's grantmaking responsive, NCRP wants to know, to *all* segments of the community, particularly the disadvantaged and disenfranchised?

The NCRP is in the midst of conducting an ongoing study of the nation's largest community foundations to answer that very question *(National Committee for Responsive Grantmaking, 1991)*. The results have sparked discussion in the field concerning the balances to be struck among different segments of the community that the community foundation is to serve.

Pluralism. Because board members are to be drawn from the diversity of the community and because geographic communities are increasingly diverse, a legal mandate for pluralism exists in the operations of its community foundation. As is the case with many institutions, living this mandate is less common than quoting it.

James Joseph, president of the Council on Foundations, cites "promoting pluralism in philanthropy" as a key implication, "if the social transformations of the future are to facilitate rather than stifle the community foundation movement" *(Joseph, 1989(b))*.

Bothwell (1989) points out that honoring diversity is written into IRS regulations for community foundations. "The regulations call for a representative governing body that represents the broad interests of the public rather than the personal or private interests of a limited number of donors."

Ylvisaker (1989) notes that "our cultural and community institutions, and particularly their governance, have not progressed as rapidly to reflect the community's burgeoning diversity."

But one thing is clear, according to Neal Peirce, syndicated newspaper columnist who is a consistent champion of "community" and a friendly critic of community foundations:

> "Community has to be at the heart of society. The influx of cultures makes it necessary. The degree of poverty and alienation in our communities makes this work necessary, the lack of understanding between groups makes it necessary. We have to expand our sense of community. The work to re-weave our social fabric has to be done in communities." *(Peirce, 1992)*.

Community foundations explore these themes when they gather for their annual meetings, where presenters, participants in panel discussions, and workshop leaders grapple with the day-to-day and year-to-year implications of running a community institution.

Community foundations and community vitality

The vitality of communities can be enhanced through the work of their community foundations. This can happen when community foundations develop productive links to other groups and institutions working to enhance the quality of community life.

But what about community foundations that don't yet have those links in place? They haven't reached the point where they can or do play an effective community leadership role. Such foundations may have financial resources, and their boards and staffs may wish to play a productive role, but because these foundations aren't connected to these different segments, very little progress is made.

The goal of community foundations bent on service to their communities must be to develop their capacities in ways that permit these useful connections to take place. With their threefold role of fund development, grantmaking, and convening, the foundation is positioned to work in tandem with committed sectors of the community.

Through *fund development,* the foundation becomes an organizational vehicle for individuals and institutions to channel and focus community resources. Through *grantmaking,* the foundation confers grants or loans in support of community building activity. Through *convening and other leadership activities,* the foundation brings people together to discuss, plan, and implement strategies. By developing its *own* capacity, the community foundation readies itself to work in partnership.

An excellent illustration of how this happens is afforded by an in-depth view of the design, operation, and results of the Leadership Program for Community Foundations. This program, designed to give small community foundations the opportunity to develop capacity, has been highly successful. The next chapter explores this Program in detail.

Chapter Two

The Leadership Program for Community Foundations

In this chapter, we introduce the Leadership Program for
Community Foundations, a program designed to put a
select group of smaller community foundations on a
fast track to enhance their capacity and efforts.
We outline the origin of this program, as well as its
design, goals, objectives, and the roles of key players.

Origins and development of the "Leadership Program for Community Foundations"

The outline for the Leadership Program for Community Foundations originated in 1986 with staff at the Ford Foundation. The Ford Foundation, then the largest foundation in the country with assets of over $6 billion and active grants throughout the nation and much of the world, knew that to be effective at the local level it could not rely on its own New York-based knowledge. Staff had observed that efforts that were not based in local leadership fared poorly for lack of local support and commitment.

Community foundations, Ford staff observed (Brown, 1993), had compelling strengths as prospective partners. First, they appeared to know their own communities well. Second, they could respond to the needs of those communities with sensitivity. Third, many of the small community foundations seemed to have unrealized potential. They were good at making small grants to a variety of institutions, but they did not appear to be very strategic grantmakers and many tended to fund established institutions rather than new experimental projects. In addition, their boards, which most often had the responsibility for selecting grantees, tended to be homogeneous and did not reflect the community's diversity. Moreover, community foundations usually lacked the staff and financial resources that would enable them to develop original and focused programs.

As Ford staff saw it, more community foundations could be encouraged to play a leadership role in their communities. They could act as a neutral convener for different and sometimes conflicting interests in a community. They could play a catalytic role by putting symbolic funds into controversial projects. Finally, like the Ford Foundation itself, they could stress the importance of diversity on the boards and staff of organizations they funded. The Ford Foundation, staff believed, could play a critical role in fostering such activities.

Earlier, in 1982, Ford had a successful experience with community foundations, joining with 15 of them to collaborate on the problem of teenage pregnancy. Ford decided to build further on the growing capacity of "locally owned and operated" community foundations to do what Ford could not do from New York City. This theme, in which community foundations are seen as local funding partners, emerged within Ford as an important motivator to create the Leadership Program.

In their background research, Ford staff identified a number of barriers that inhibit the effectiveness of community foundations.

Few financial resources. The major barrier was the large number of community foundations with very little in the way of assets. More than 220 of the approximately 300 community foundations identified in a 1984 survey by the Council on Foundations had assets below $5 million. Staff wrote *(Ford Foundation, 1986)*, "First and most simply, community foundations of this size need additional assets. Experts note that once a community foundation accumulates about $10 million, its growth takes off markedly. An endowment of this size establishes a credibility and stability that attracts additional donors and provides sufficient income to achieve economy of scale in the community foundation's operation. A big factor in this growth is the ability to support additional full-time staff, usually an expansion from one to two professionals. Thus, an accelerated infusion of capital to help a community foundation reach the 'take-off' point can substantially reduce the time it takes for it to become a significant community force."

Even fewer discretionary financial resources. "A second
need of small community foundations is for discretionary, permanent assets. For small community foundations facing the pressure
to grow, the 'easiest' money to raise is money with the most
strings attached, donor advised or designated funds. Many donors
are not yet fully confident in the small community foundation as a
competent institution. Therefore, rather than make a discretionary
gift, they often prefer to earmark their funds for particular grantees
such as the local hospital or symphony. Discretionary funds, however, are those that enable the community foundation to respond
most flexibly to local needs as they change over time."

Little experience with community leadership. Finally, many
community foundations had not fully developed or even explored
their potential as community leadership institutions. Many viewed
their role solely as responding to grant requests "rather than, for
example, providing a neutral place for diverse constituencies to
problem-solve on important community issues, encouraging collaborative public-private ventures, engaging in public education,
or playing an important social entrepreneurial role . . . Finally,
small community foundations often have limited capacity to develop a carefully targeted, multi-year grantmaking strategy to
respond to the most pressing needs of the community. Most foundations of this size have only one professional staff person whose
primary job is to increase the assets of the foundation. Limited
staff time and program experience combined with few discretionary funds can result in a large number of very small grants that
may not reflect the priorities of the community. Simply raising
new assets and responding to requests for funds tends to consume all of the staff time. It is also very difficult for a community
foundation with only one staff person to assume a leadership role
helping the community ascertain its priority needs, let alone develop strategies to address them."

Design of the Program

The Leadership Program for Community Foundations was designed to overcome these three barriers[1]. A brief prepared by Ford Foundation staff reveals how the objectives of the Program could respond most directly to the three major barriers to capacity development.

"The proposed initiative would encourage a select group of community foundations to assume leadership roles in shaping local responses to important problems facing their communities. It is based on a growing consensus regarding the needs of small community foundations, in particular, those with assets below $10 million.

"The proposed initiative would be structured to meet these needs. It would help community foundations leverage new discretionary endowment funds while providing support for the development and implementation of a five-year grants program targeting an important community problem of the foundation's choice. The assumption is that by exercising leadership in addressing an important community problem, community foundations can gain visibility and additional legitimacy

---

1 While not the first big private foundation to support community foundations, Ford staff worked with a small group of advisors and listened to pioneers and spokespeople for the field, and learned from the experience of other private foundations that had supported community foundations.

Foremost was the Charles Stewart Mott Foundation, which has invested tens of millions of dollars in administrative and endowment support, technical assistance programs, and programmatic initiatives for community foundations. Another is the David and Lucille Packard Foundation which granted $3.1 million in a challenge grant program that encouraged community foundations in the Bay Area of California to develop permanent endowment. Still another is the Gannett Foundation which provided $25,000 grants to new or revitalizing community foundations in 30 communities in which the Gannett Corporation had operations.

After the Leadership Program was underway, the Lilly Endowment began an initiative to help grow and strengthen community foundations throughout Indiana. The Rockefeller Foundation and W.K. Kellogg Foundation also began initiatives to strengthen the leadership role of community foundations in support of children's issues. In addition to these official programs of support, dozens of private foundations also have made grants to community foundations in their regions to support operations, to help operate a grantmaking program, or to help build an endowment.

as well as attract new donors while providing an important community service. The goal of the proposed five-year initiative would be to leave the participating community foundations with increased assets for flexible grantmaking as well an enhanced staff capacity and commitment to assuming a leadership role in community problem-solving.

"Ford's grant would give the community foundation the capacity to spend $100,000 annually for five years to cover the costs of carrying out a grants program targeting a problem selected by the community to be of substantial community importance. Such costs could include both the program grants and administrative/staff costs incurred in developing, implementing and evaluating the program. In this way, the Ford grant would address both a program and asset development goal."

A group of advisors (see Appendix A), led by Tom Beech, formerly executive director of The Minneapolis Foundation, helped staff shape the Program, and later, review aplications.

Goals and objectives

The Leadership Program for Community Foundations was aimed at sustained capacity-building among community foundations. Specifically, it was designed to assist a group of community foundations to play leadership roles in shaping local responses to important problems facing their communities and to accelerate the growth in these foundations' discretionary endowments so they can become more significant forces in their respective communities.

There were essentially two objectives for participants. The first was one of community leadership — to enable a participating community foundation to play a leadership role in addressing an important community problem for which it did not currently have sufficient resources.

As intended by the Program's sponsors, participants were to practice the full range of community leadership skills that were, at the time, cutting edge approaches in community philanthropy:

(1) developing and implementing a grants program that focused on a selected problem and combined a long-term preventive and policy-oriented perspective with a response to immediate service needs as appropriate;

(2) convening diverse constituents, including bringing together different ideas and points of view, facilitating learning and dialogue on important issues, and fostering the sense and reality of community;

(3) acting as a catalyst, including encouraging collaborative philanthropy, providing seed money and leveraging funds, taking initiative on challenging issues, and facilitating public-private ventures.

The second objective was one of fund development — to assist participating foundations in enlarging their discretionary endowments and to provide the necessary momentum for sustained growth. The Ford Foundation awarded grants of $500,000 to community foundations selected competitively in response to the Foundation's Program Announcement and Application. Participating community foundations would seek new assets to match these grants on a two-to-one basis (i.e., $1 million) with discretionary endowment funds. The Program's expectations:

(1) Participating community foundations were required to raise $1 million within the first two years of the Program. Funds had to be in-hand or committed to delivery within the five years of the Program to qualify. All matching funds were to be assigned to permanent discretionary or broadly defined field-of-interest endowment.

(2) Assuming the matching requirements were met, the Leadership Program's $500,000 grant was to be paid out to each participating foundation within the first two years of the

Program. The first $100,000 was advanced at the beginning of the first year, and was to be expended in the first year to mount the leadership initiative.

(3) It was expected that the $500,000 would be spent by participating foundations in annual amounts of $100,000 for program grants and administrative/staff expenses over the five years of the Leadership Program. However, no more than $50,000 per year could be used to support the administration of the program.

(4) At their option, participating community foundations could raise additional funds from local sources for the grants program. Foundations that successfully pursued this option could transfer a like amount of the Leadership Program grant each year (up to $50,000) into endowment. This optional incentive was designed to attract private foundations, corporations, and other local donors who would not be likely to contribute to the community foundation's endowment but who would be interested in helping the community foundation work on a substantial problem facing the community.

Three rounds of participants

At first, $4 million was provided to eight small community foundations (See Box: Participants) whose applications were carefully reviewed against a set of criteria. Targeted community foundations were those with permanent assets of no less than $2 million and no more than $10 million. Pre-grant site visits to applicants determined whether there was sufficient capacity in the foundation to mount a meaningful initiative and whether there was sufficient community support behind the foundation's proposal.

Within a few months after a kick-off meeting in New York for all participants, and after a round of visits to each site by the project director and the program evaluator, it was evident that there was

Participants[2]

Leadership Program for Community Foundations

Round One (1987-1991)
Arizona Community Foundation
Dade Community Foundation
The Dayton Foundation
El Paso Community Foundation
Community Foundation of Greater Greenville
Community Foundation of Greater Memphis
Rochester Area Foundation
Community Foundation for Southeastern Michigan

Round Two (1989-1993)
Baltimore Community Foundation
The Community Foundation for Greater Lorain County
Madison Community Foundation
Greater New Orleans Foundation
Central New York Community Foundation
Foundation Northwest
The Community Foundation Serving Richmond and
    Central Virginia
East Tennessee Foundation
Greater Triangle Community Foundation
Tucson Community Foundation

Round Three (1991-1995)
Delaware Community Foundation
Duluth-Superior Area Community Foundation
Fargo-Moorhead Area Foundation
The Community Foundation of Greater Greensboro
Maine Community Foundation
Rockford Community Trust
Sacramento Regional Foundation
Community Foundation of Greater Santa Cruz County
Vermont Community Foundation

---

2 For a full listing of community foundation names, addresses and their
directors, see Appendix B.

sufficient merit to the model and sufficient progress among participants that Ford considered offering a second round of grants to a
new set of participants.

This consideration was aided by the possibility that the John D.
and Catherine T. MacArthur Foundation would join as a partner.
Their support allowed the extension of participation to 10 additional community foundations, plus smaller "developmental
grants" to a number of applicants with promising but not quite
winning proposals.

A few relatively minor changes were made to the eligibility requirements and the application process. The target group shifted
slightly to those community foundations with permanent assets
of no less than $3 million and not more than $13 million. But the
major features of the Program were unchanged: the dual focus on
asset development and program leadership; the five-year program
scope; the two-year matching requirement; an allotment for administration and technical assistance; site visits to articulate "lessons
learned" and publications to distribute them; and annual meetings
among participants to discuss insights on successes and difficulties
in growth and development.

A new program announcement and application, now describing a
"joint initiative of the Ford and MacArthur Foundations," went out in
January 1988, and 10 community foundations were chosen for full
participation, beginning January 1, 1989 (ending December 31, 1993).

Even with 18 participants, the program's sponsors recognized that
there were still community foundations that could benefit from the
program, and a third round was announced in 1990, also as a joint
initiative of the Ford and MacArthur Foundations. Nine additional
community foundations were chosen to begin in January 1991 and
end December 1995, bringing the total number of participants to 27.

Typologies or stage models to describe community foundation
growth have been developed by two observers of the community
foundation field. These writers would agree that participants in
this Program were, when selected, somewhere in the middle

range of their growth curves. Leonard *(1989)* describes three stages, Stage I: New, revitalizing, and first-generation foundations; Stage II: Maturing foundations; Stage III: Mature foundations. In Stevens' *(1993)* "life cycles of nonprofit organizations," Program participants fell into the Growth Stage ("an organization whose services are established in the marketplace but whose operations are not yet stabilized"). While all were in a growth mode at the time of their selection, the purpose of the Program was to *accelerate* that growth in capacity.

The role of the project director

The implementation of all three Rounds and the provision of ongoing support services to participants was managed from outside the Ford Foundation by Barrie Pribyl, former director of the New York Regional Association of Grantmakers and a consultant to philanthropic and nonprofit efforts. A grant from Ford to Community Resource Exchange, a New York-based nonprofit organization that provides management assistance to other nonprofits, supported her efforts.

Each January the project director convened a two-day gathering of each Round's participants. Two people, typically the executive director, board chair, and occasionally a key program officer from each participating community foundation were invited. These meetings were designed to allow participants to share news and insights of their progress in capacity building, as well as to explore a number of timely topics in depth. Outside resource people were often invited to present material or facilitate discussion.

Pribyl maintained regular contact with each participant in several ways: visiting sites, monitoring their progress and as needed, offering supportive consultation, facilitating access to additional resources, and identifying opportunities for information sharing with other participants.

The project director visited each of the participating community foundations during the first year of its participation in the Program. These day-long visits enabled the project director to see firsthand how plans for their asset development and program initiative were taking shape and to identify opportunities for technical assistance from the Program. Additional visits were made by special arrangement throughout the duration of the Leadership Program.

A pool of funds was created by the Ford Foundation and managed by the director specifically to support "technical assistance" to participants. Participants were encouraged to imagine how they could use such funds productively to support their development and to submit a simple request to the project director.

The role of the program evaluator

Evaluation goals were pursued by Rainbow Research[3] through a grant from the Ford Foundation. Chief among them was to increase the body of knowledge available to the entire field of community foundations and philanthropy on successful strategies of community foundation development. This book is the culmination of that effort, supplementing the publication of three annual magazines *(Rainbow Research, Inc. 1989, 1990, 1991)*.

The role of Rainbow Research was not to evaluate the success or performance of the different participating community foundations, but to learn how they grew and developed given this opportunity. The field is young enough, diverse enough, and reflective enough to be very much in a "discovery mode" and to defy the imposition of performance standards. The premise of these evaluation efforts was that each community foundation would develop in response to local conditions. There could be as many "paths to effectiveness" as there were participating community foundations. These

---

3 Rainbow Research, Inc., is a Minneapolis-based nonprofit organization whose mission is "to assist socially concerned organizations respond more effectively to community problems and opportunities." Two of its principal strategies are program evaluation and program improvement products and services.

are likely to have enough similarities from which to draw preliminary principles, and enough uniqueness to respect as legitimate variation.

To guide the discovery of effectiveness and how it evolves in young, growing community foundations, Rainbow Research developed a framework that allowed monitoring of growth and development in four major categories, which in turn broke down into twelve (See Box: *Overview of areas for evaluation*). These had emerged as "growth factors" in the development of community foundation in the author's earlier studies *(Mayer, 1988)*.

Data were collected by three principal means:

Site visits. Rainbow Research staff visited each participating community foundation in Rounds One and Two during the first, second, and fifth years of their participation. The first visit was primarily to introduce participants to the Areas for Evaluation, and to their possibilities for self-evaluation and self-reflection. The visits during Year Two and Year Five were for two days each, in which we met with board, staff, advisors/volunteers, grant recipients, partners to local initiatives, and knowledgeable bystanders without direct involvement in the community foundation's activities[4].

Artifacts and commentaries. Rainbow Research staff kept up with developments among participants through receipt of their public materials (newsletters and annual reports), as well as private materials (new policies and guidelines), and through contacts at professional meetings and by phone.

Annual surveys. As Rainbow Research and participants became more sure of the Areas for Evaluation and of the dimensions for

---

4 Round Three participants were not visited by the program evaluator. The sponsor's wish to get findings into the field before they became obsolete suggested that this synthesis be written just as Round Two was finishing up, when Round One had been finished for two years, but two years before Round Three would finish. Growth data were collected by survey from Round Three participants, some of which are used in this book, notably in Chapter Four.

Overview of areas for evaluation

Organizational development

Administration: Strengthened administration and staffing of the community foundation.

Board: Board functioning that increasingly serves the development of the community foundation's mission, organizational capacity, financial assets, and programs.

Staff: Staff complement with enhanced skills and support to address the issue area chosen for this program.

Asset development

Endowment growth: A fund development strategy that allows the community foundation to grow as quickly as possible.

Communications: Increased visibility and attractiveness of the community foundation in appropriate segments of the community, and vice versa.

Administrative support: Increased financial support and broadened base of financial support.

Community role

Leadership skills: Increased expertise in the variety of roles that a community foundation can play in addressing a community issue.

Contribution to progress: Increased focus, momentum, legitimacy, and support given to addressing the issue area.

Institutional linkages: Strengthened relationships between the community foundation and different segments of the community, and strengthened relationships among different segments.

Programming and grantmaking

Grantmaking procedures: Effective grantmaking practices.

Strategic grantmaking: A "portfolio" of grants or projects conducive to achieving impact in the community foundation's chosen issue area.

Programming effectiveness: Strengthened approaches to other issue areas experienced by the community.

41

data collection, an annual survey grew from two questions to a substantial notebook. These produced data concerning current practices, used in discussion at participants' annual meetings.

Rather than wait five years for the Program's conclusion to produce a set of usable findings, Rainbow Research and Ford created an annual series of publications. This magazine, named *CF/Findings from the Leadership Program for Community Foundations* was inspired by *Inc./The Magazine for Growing Small Businesses* and was designed in a popular format meant to be digestible by even the busiest board member. Two issues were produced each year — one on resource development and institutional growth, and one on community leadership — for three years, and were distributed throughout the community foundation field. They proved to be especially useful to those foundations interested in applying to Round Two when it was announced, and then later to Round Three, as a means of transferring the techniques and wisdom that were being developed and formulated by the earlier "pioneers."

Chapter Three

Taking on Capacity:
Resource Development

In this chapter, we begin our exploration of the results
and lessons learned through the Leadership Program for
Community Foundations. This chapter focuses specifically
on the area of resource development. We examine why
discretionary financial resources are so important and
highlight the growth achieved by Program participants.
Also detailed are three phases of financial growth that
Program participants experienced, and the major strategies
they have pursued in developing their financial resources.

Financial resources:
A key ingredient of capacity[1]

"Resources" are a key ingredient of community capacity, as discussed in Chapter One. Chief among resources are financial resources.

The very purpose of a community foundation is to accumulate financial resources that can be deployed in the service of its community. The financial resources held by a community foundation are indeed "community capital."

The small amount of discretionary resources typically held by community foundations limit their ability to play a more active leadership role. Large community foundations typically fare little better in this respect than small ones. The collection of funds held by a community foundation, large or small, varies in the degree of participation the donor plays in making recommendations for grant-making. The box on page 47 reveals some distinctions in a community foundation's "chart of accounts."

---

1 The astute reader will notice our chapter order — resources, commitment, skills — does not parallel the order of capacity ingredients cited in Chapter One: commitment, resources, skills. In fact, a mobilization of commitment began with potential applicants to this Program even before they were selected, as they prepared their case to its sponsors, as discussed in Chapter Four. But because resource development was a primary goal of this Program as well as the initial focus of all community foundations once they began their participation, it is discussed first here.

So-called "discretionary funds" and broadly stated "field-of-interest funds" come from donors that expressly acknowledge the foundation's expertise in formulating priorities and guidelines for use of charitable dollars in ways it sees fit, as community needs and opportunities emerge over time. But these discretionary funds are typically the most scarce in a community foundation's holdings. More common are funds in which the donor plays a significant role in formulating recommendations for grantmaking. While the interests of donors may coincide with the priorities of the foundation, this cannot be assumed.

Development of discretionary resources: A goal for Leadership Program participants

Increasing the discretionary funds which a community foundation can use to implement its own priorities was a major motive of the Ford Foundation. Its Leadership Program for Community Foundations was designed to help those community foundations that want to take a more active leadership role in focusing philanthropic resources to help their communities address problems.

Each community foundation chosen for participation was given $500,000 over five years *if* it raised pledges for $1 million in new, permanent discretionary, or broad field-of-interest funds in the first two years.

The remainder of this chapter discusses the results of that resource development effort. It presents results as reflected in the growth of participants' endowments, as well as their capacity to increase their endowments. It also presents the strategies they pursued to make the match and the strategies they began to employ in the service of longer-term growth goals.

Community foundation funds

Permanent and Non-permanent funds: A permanent fund (also called an endowment fund) created in a community foundation to provide income which will be used for charitable purposes. Some funds held by community foundations are non-permanent, or "in-and-out" funds; typically the principal is distributed as grants. The funds described below can come in permanent or non-permanent form.

Designated fund: A component fund whose beneficiaries have been specified by a donor or the governing board. Examples include a fund maintained by a community foundation to support the local chapter of the American Red Cross or a fund to support the basketball program of the local Boys/ Girls Club. Such funds may be named for the agency or the donor. Sometimes the designated agency contributes to its own open-ended fund while at other times third parties may establish and contribute to these funds.

Donor-advised fund: A fund which is formally structured to enable the donor to suggest specific grants *ad hoc*. Such recommendations are not binding but are taken into consideration when grants are awarded. One such example is a fund established by a living donor who will, from time to time, meet with the staff and/or selected board members to suggest possible grants.

Field-of-interest fund: A component fund established to support a particular cause, geographic area, or population to be benefited by the grant funds. Donors do not specify which agencies receive assistance; the governing board has full discretion. Examples include a fund for the arts; a fund for programs serving disadvantaged youth; and a fund for energy conservation efforts by nonprofit agencies. A broad field-of-interest fund has broader focus, such as the arts, youth or energy, though a donor may narrow the focus of a particular donation.

Discretionary fund: A component fund which has no external restrictions on its use or purposes, and can be used for any purpose designated by the governing board.

Results: Growth in financial resources

Participating community foundations experienced growth in phases. In fact, two or three different phases of resource development took place during the five years of this Program. There was usually overlap rather than a clear demarcation of these three phases at each site, and the duration of each phase also varied from site to site.

In the first two years, participants focused on making the match, i.e., in raising the required $1 million. In the second phase, the match-making efforts lessened, and were replaced with a consolidation of growth in the areas of internal administration, program development and community leadership — mostly occasioned by the first phase of rapid growth. The third phase saw a build up of certain elements of resource development infrastructure needed for long-term growth.

Highlights for Round One participants[2]

Figure 3-1 shows the growth in permanent funds for Round One from the time participants entered the Program in January 1987 until the time they ended five years later. It also reveals the proportion of those funds that is discretionary.

- Round One participants grew from an average of $9 million in permanent funds to an average of $22 million.

- This represents growth of 141 percent (more than double), or an average growth rate of almost 20 percent per year.

---

2 Variations in accounting practices make comparisons across community foundations difficult. Not all observe the same fiscal year. Many participants changed their fiscal year during their time in the Program. Most changed their accounting practices as well. Perhaps most important, there is variation as to whether or not supporting organizations are reported as part of the assets of the foundation, and variation in considering those funds discretionary. Those last two points serve to underrepresent the assets and their classification in this report.

Figure 3-1

Total Permanent Funds
All Eight Community Foundations in Round One

January 1987 through December 1991

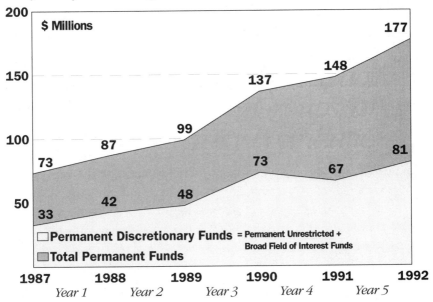

- Two community foundations more than doubled their permanent endowment (Southeastern Michigan and Dayton), two others more than tripled (Rochester and Arizona), and one more than quadrupled (El Paso).

- The largest foundation at the beginning (Dayton) remained the largest, and the smallest at the beginning (Greenville) remained the smallest. Otherwise there was considerable re-ordering.

- Round One grew its discretionary endowment from an average of $4.12 million to an average of $10.12 million.

- This represents growth of 145 percent, or an average growth rate of 21 percent per year.

- At the beginning, an average of 45 percent of permanent endowment was made up of discretionary funds; by the end, this had only slightly increased to 46 percent.

- Five community foundations more than doubled their discretionary endowment (Dade, Dayton, El Paso, Greenville, and Southeastern Michigan), one more than tripled (Rochester), and one more than quadrupled (Arizona).

Some years were better than others; this varied by site. Also, no two growth curves were alike (see Figure 3-2). For discretionary funds, the third year's growth rate was best (53 percent), with an average of 21 percent for the first two years. Year Four showed a decrease of 8 percent for the group, as three participants reclassified funds from discretionary to non-discretionary, undertaken as part of their financial re-tooling. Year Five showed an average growth rate of 50 percent, largely due to a huge increase at one site (Dayton); three others showed losses through re-classification that year. In other words, Figure 3-1 is a composite view that obscures site differences.

Figure 3-2
Total Permanent Funds
Round One Participants: January 1987 through December 1991

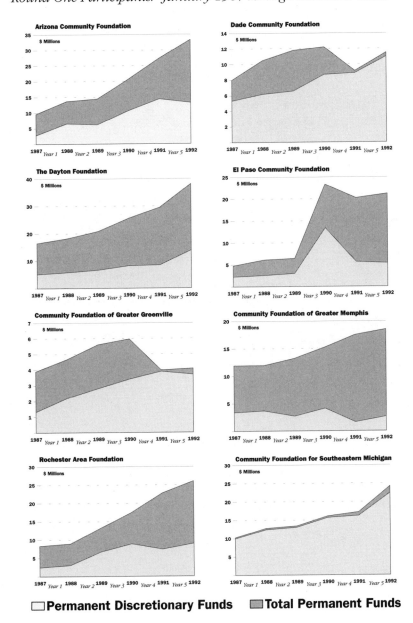

Permanent Discretionary Funds　　**Total Permanent Funds**

Highlights for Round Two participants

Figure 3-3 shows the same data for Round Two for its five years in the Program, beginning January 1989 and ending December 1993.

Figure 3-3

Total Permanent Funds
All Ten Community Foundations in Round Two

January 1989 through December 1993

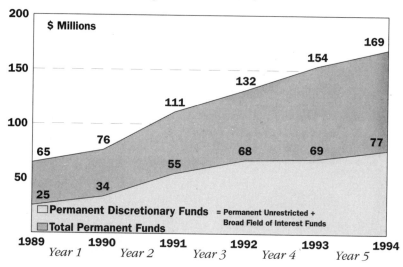

- Round Two participants grew from an average of $6.5 million in permanent funds to an average of $16.9 million. (Round Two participants started with an average permanent endowment 72 percent the size of Round One at its start and finished 77 percent the size of Round One at the end of their five years).

- This represents growth of 160 percent (more than double), or an average growth rate of almost 22 percent per year.

- Six community foundations more than doubled their permanent endowment (Baltimore, Lorain, New Orleans, Central New York, Richmond, East Tenneessee), and two more than quadrupled (Madison, Tucson).

- The largest foundation at the beginning was not the largest at the end, and the smallest at the beginning was not the smallest at the end. There was considerable re-ordering.

- Growth in discretionary funds (208 percent, more than tripling) was greater than for total funds (160 percent).

- Round Two grew its discretionary endowment from an average of $2.5 million to an average of $7.7 million.

- Six community foundations more than doubled their discretionary endowment (Baltimore, Lorain, Central New York, Richmond, East Tenneessee, Tucson), one more than tripled (Triangle), and one more than quadrupled (Madison).

- At the beginning, an average of 38 percent of permanent endowment was made up of discretionary funds (compared to 45 percent in Round One). By the end of Year Five, this had increased to 46 percent, comparable to Round One.

Figure 3-4
Total Permanent Funds

Round Two Participants: January 1989 through December 1993

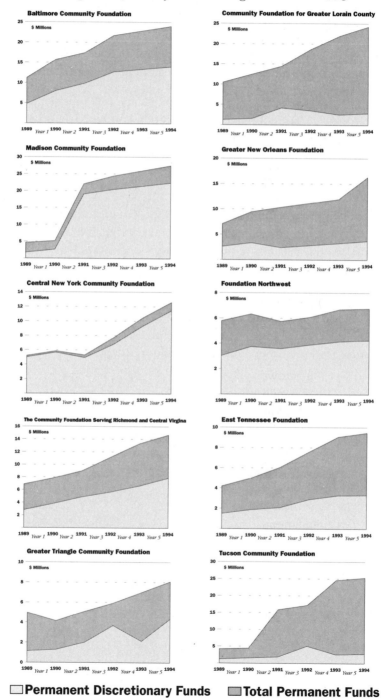

☐ **Permanent Discretionary Funds**   ■ **Total Permanent Funds**

54

Growth phase one: Responding to a match requirement

All participants raised the required $1 million by the two-year deadline. Several made it within one year, and several received much more than the match. Considering all types of permanent funds — not only the required discretionary or broad field-of-interest funds — this is what they raised for permanent endowment, on average, during their first two years:

- The eight Round One participants took in a total of $25.7 million in new permanent endowment, for an average of $3.2 million. There was some variation across the eight, ranging from $1.3 million to $4.8 million, and the median was $3.5 million.

- The ten Round Two participants took in a total of $46.5 million, for an average of $4.6 million. Here there was much greater variation, partly because two participants took in more than $10 million (through a bequest and new supporting organizations), and three participants, while later refining their chart of accounts, re-classified some of their receipts from the first two years from permanent to non-permanent. The range in two-year growth, after re-classification, was from essentially zero to $17.5 million, and the median was $3.5 million in new permanent endowment.

Strategy and context for making the match

In raising these new funds, most participants pursued two major strategies simultaneously. One was a concerted effort by board members to solicit "large gifts" ($10,000 to $100,000) from a list of prospects drawn up specifically for the purpose of making the match. The other was a concerted effort by staff to communicate the mission and the story of the community foundation much more broadly and deeply in the community than ever before.

Two other things happened concurrently. First, foundations took the opportunity to do some serious planning. Board members who acted boldly in seeking nominees for the prospect list needed assurance that the foundation was clear about its mission, its policies and practices, its programs, and how endowments were used and managed. While the product — the written plan with goals and action steps — was important, what mattered more was the agreement between the board and staff.

Second, each foundation launched its "community initiative" in a substantive area of its choice. The second major goal of the Program for its participants — along with increasing discretionary funds — was the development of community leadership skills needed to play a more meaningful role in community problem solving. Participants were encouraged to convene diverse community constituencies and make grants that would spur progress in their chosen area. Most participants carried out their resource development work within the context of these initiatives. That is, they prepared to tell their prospective donors, "This is an example of what a community foundation can do when it has discretionary resources."

- While most participants undertook a concerted effort, they avoided the term "campaign." A campaign, they noted, is how *other* types of nonprofit institutions raise money — usually noisy and visible efforts to reach a broad constituency. Participants in this Program favored quiet and discreet efforts, in which board members and staff called on a small, well-chosen group of individuals. At the same time, they geared up their communications to publicize their initiative, their hard-won status as a participant in the Leadership Program for Community Foundations, and their growing role in the community in behalf of donors large and small. Both efforts paid off.

A small number of participants avoided undertaking anything different from the resource development strategies of their recent past, and their efforts succeeded as well.

Sources of gifts to endowment: A special study

A special study was done as part of this evaluation, with data received from Round Two participants during the first 20 months of their participation. They recorded gifts to endowment — received or pledged — whether discretionary, broad field-of-interest, donor-advised, or donor-designated. All new permanent gifts were included — not just those that counted towards the match.

Table 3-1 shows the basic facts regarding these sources of gifts.

Table 3-1
Sources of Gifts to Permanent Endowment

Source	$ Amount	Percent	No. Gifts
Living individuals	3,805,641	20.4	612
Corporations	4,448,597	23.8	113
Agencies, pooled funds, etc.	4,621,962	24.8	102
Foundations	4,025,137	21.6	66
Other	1,755,543	9.5	25
Total	**18,656,880**	**100**	**918**

Individuals. Individuals, making 612 gifts to the 10 community foundations in Round Two, made up these community foundations' largest donor base, even though the dollar value of their gifts is less than those from other sources. Two-thirds of all gifts came from individuals, constituting 20.4 percent of the value of all gifts. At any one foundation, gifts from individuals varied from 10 percent to 60 percent. The median gift from individuals across all foundations was $1,000. In other words, *half the gifts to endowment were $1,000 or less, the other half were more.* These data have important implications for resource development strategy, since development minded boards and staff typically solicit wealthy individuals for substantial gifts.

Corporations. The conventional wisdom at the time this Program was designed was that corporations do not give to endowment. Not only did it prove untrue, but corporations played a significant role at virtually every foundation.

Agency endowments, pooled funds, and more. Generally, these donations are pools of money designated for specific uses. Most often they originate outside the foundation, and are then integrated within it. Agency endowments are the most common example. Some community foundations seek them out because administration of these funds is a useful and visible community service, and because the foundation can (though not all do) charge a fee for its service, providing revenue to its administrative budget. Scholarship funds and memorial funds are also included in this category.

Foundations. Foundations, principally local ones, played a significant role in contributing to these foundations' resource development efforts during the study period. The median gift from foundations was substantial: $25,000. All participants but one received at least one foundation gift, and one received 23. Not all these gifts were grants. Some were transfers of resources to the community foundation upon termination of their status as a private foundation. Attitudes among community foundation directors differ on the advisability of persuading private foundations to transfer their resources. Most are in favor of it as a strategy for increasing the size of the foundation, but others feel that local philanthropy is better served by a multitude of independent foundations.

"Other." The remaining 9.5 percent of gifts (by value) were contributed by (a) bequests, (b) anonymous donors and (c) miscellaneous. There were six bequests during the twenty-month study period. Bequests, it is often said, are the source of long-term growth for foundations. Yet because of the Program's match requirement to raise $1 million within two short years, efforts to develop bequests were often put on the back burner until the match was met.

No "one best way"

A major finding of the Program is that there is no "one best way" to develop financial resources — not even for the short term. This is shown in the different growth curves in Figures 3-1, 3-2, 3-3, and 3-4, as well as the different sources of revenue from their efforts.

Even though each community foundation had a plan for raising the required $1 million in discretionary funds, the plan was seldom implemented in all its detail, and its eventual fruits were only barely imagined.

Gifts came from all fronts, and many came as a surprise. Anticipated gifts often didn't materialize; many gifts came from unexpected sources; and many substantial gifts were completely unanticipated. This is not to say that planning didn't help — it helped enormously. But it does show that even with the best laid plans, the outcome cannot be foreseen.

One conclusion is that growing quickly requires multiple growth strategies — multiple prospects of multiple types, multiple "pitches" that appeal to multiple audiences, and multiple avenues of communication. At the outset, not one community foundation could have guessed that the profile of gifts to endowment would turn out as it did.

Long-lasting effects

The activities required to make the match had some very important effects:

Board members greatly increased their commitment to the institution. Board members pulled together as a team and put together a successful resource development effort, built up the infrastructure of their institution, enjoyed the greater visibility that an important matching grant and community leadership initiative gave them, and relished the discretion in grantmaking that holding more discretionary funds would give them. The energizing of the board was an essential ingredient to success with making the match and with developing a longer range vision of development.

Staff created the elements of a resource development "machine." Efforts launched at the beginning of the Program (and even before that) continued to bring in funds long after the match was raised. These included communications strategies, strengthened relationships with more sectors of the donor community and their advisors, and protocols for monitoring donor activity and accounts.

Community foundations extended and reached into niches that have proved productive. Participants made themselves visible to many more kinds of donors, community-minded people and institutions, and potential public and private partners from nearby and beyond. Most community foundations found they could negotiate a useful role for themselves that had favorable implications for resource development (as well as for programming and community leadership).

At many foundations these effects endured long after the match was made, helping them to move into long-range resource development efforts. At others, these pieces needed to be re-established after a period of relative inactivity before moving to the next level.

Growth phase two: Transition from short-term goals to long-term vision

Participants were told early and often that making the match was the beginning, not the end, of their resource development work. Raising $1 million in response to the match requirement of the Program was the only formal requirement, a short-term goal intended to create long-term vision and efforts. Making the match was to help participants build the resource development infrastructure. This would support them in the task of more sustained development efforts that would serve larger, long-range goals.

Immediately after making the match, however, almost all participants took a break from the rigors of resource development. Several foundations had expended their biggest effort near the deadline to make the match, and were exhausted. Others relied on raising the last dollars from their own board members, who wished not to be asked for anything more, especially money, at least not for a while. For others, new demands intruded on the feeling of victory.

This is not to say they were idle. Rather, Years Three and Four of their participation in the Program focused more on strengthening different areas of internal administration and the community initiative — topics explored in the next two chapters. Fortunately, even though they relaxed their efforts to raise discretionary resources during this hiatus, the growth curves show that earlier work continued to have an effect.

The role of "planned giving" in long term growth

In making the match, participants learned two important principles: (1) rapid resource development *can* be done, and (2) you don't get what you don't ask for. These two principles are well known to seasoned fundraisers, and were experienced directly and re-affirmed by those in the Program.

Participants also saw that big-time growth was unlikely to come from the relatively small gifts attracted in response to the match requirement. Those gifts were important for adding to the here-and-now capability of the foundation to further a community initiative and their own institutional development. They also were important for beginning a relationship with a host of new donors.

Those gifts were small, relatively speaking. Only 7 percent of gifts from individuals were larger than $20,000 in the special study referred to in the previous section. Since people of wealth made up the lion's share of foundations' prospect lists, it became apparent that (1) much of their revenues came from small donors who were reached through their communications efforts, and (2) they were not yet tapping their prospects' real potential for giving.

In short, they saw that much of the value of those gifts lay in the relationship begun between donor and foundation. A chain of events emerged in the minds of foundation officials. In this chain, one could turn small initial gifts into larger subsequent gifts. First identify prospective donors, turn prospects into donors, and finally, turn donors into "planned givers."

In this reformulated vision for long-term growth, "planned giving" plays a central role. Planned giving is a discipline of the estate planning and financial advisory communities. It benefits from the tax advantages provided by federal tax policy to people of even modest wealth. With this approach, long-term growth comes from successfully encouraging donors to include the community foundation in their plans for generating retirement income, their plans for resource management, and their plans for estate transfer.

Planned giving is the current watchword not only with community foundations, but with many endowment building institutions. It is appealing to community foundations for two key reasons. First, it permits foundations to develop an ongoing relationship with wealthy donors and to establish themselves as donor-serving institutions. It allows foundations to develop vehicles for charitable giving designed to satisfy a variety of "philanthropic needs" apparently experienced by those with substantial resources.

It's a fact that gifts made in wills or trusts are likely to be higher, on average, than "living gifts." In the special study referred to earlier, the average living gift was $6,218 ($1,000 was the median); the average gift by bequest (there were six) was $123,666 ($28,000 was the median).

Second, planned giving, when emphasized, distinguishes the foundation from institutions that hold "annual appeals," "fundraising campaigns," or even "match-making efforts." It avoids the appearance of competition with nonprofits that campaign for annual operations and with issue-focused nonprofits that present their case directly to the public. It does not, however, avoid competition with other institutions that raise endowments, a great number of which are also now employing strategies to develop their resources through planned giving.

With planned giving as a tool for resource development, "donor education" becomes a central part of the foundation's job. As they prepare their will or establish a trust, most people enlist the help of a professional advisor, typically an estate attorney or certified public accountant. Sometimes an insurance agent or stock broker is involved. To get donors to include the foundation in these wills or trusts, the foundation must first reach the leading professional advisors in its community and persuade *them* of the merits of the community foundation as a reasonable and acceptable means — indeed, the preferred means — of satisfying their clients' philanthropic needs.

Growth phase three: Development roles for long-term growth

It took most participants a considerable time to formulate a new goal for resource growth *after* they made the match. During the annual meetings of Program participants, board chairs were encouraged to state a goal for the year 2000, and most were unflinching in their expansive estimates. Once back home, however, plans for reaching this goal were slow to gel. The time devoted to shaping up internal operations precluded planning for the launching of anything resembling a campaign-with-a-goal. Instead they concentrated on putting key pieces of the resource development machinery in place: the communications piece, the donor relations piece, the professional advisor piece, and so on.

Resource development is labor intensive work, involving several focused tasks: producing brochures for the professional advisor community that describe the merits of giving to or through the community foundation; hosting breakfasts or luncheons for professional advisors, making presentations at their firms, or meeting with them one-on-one; producing newsletters targeted to prospective donors that describe the activities of the community foundation; cultivating relationships with current donors of the foundation, interesting them in its programmatic activities and alerting them to opportunities to participate.

These duties are typically spread across several positions in a three-to-five person community foundation, but the sixth or seventh person is likely to be a "development officer," "communications officer," "donor relations officer," or a combination. Typically the executive director retains significant development and donor relations functions. This new development person is usually hired after a high level financial officer, and certainly after the institution's financial and investment management and monitoring practices are strengthened.

Including such a person in the foundation's administrative budget is always a major stretch. It can be justified, but it takes time for most boards to make the commitment to support such a person. It's not unusual to hire this person with support from outside institutions, such as nearby foundations, banks, or other stakeholders in the community foundation's growth. The cash flow projections needed to determine the feasibility of this position require organizational know-how (computer expertise, financial management skills, and financial databases that reliably reveal sources and schedules of income and expenses). Typically this level of know-how and this hiring decision are approached at about the same time in the growth curve of these community foundations.

It is exactly this plane of organizational growth and development — planning, implementing, upgrading, in rapid succession if not simultaneously, changes to several administrative systems: financial, personnel, communications, technical — that characterized

Years Three, Four, and some of Five for most participants. On another track, programmatic activities were proceeding at a rapid pace.

Below are descriptions of the variety of "development roles" that are undertaken in growing community foundations. How they are configured in different staff positions depends on the skills already present in the foundation. That is, a new development person may be hired primarily to do donor relations, or primarily for communications, depending on pre-existing division of duties.

Development role #1: Work with professional advisors

There's a key to getting the attention of prospective planned givers: getting the attention of their advisors. For an increasing number of people, this includes professional advisors such as estate attorneys, planners, CPAs, insurance underwriters, and brokers.

Forming a "professional advisors committee" that both gives advice to the community foundation and gets advice from it is a central strategy for many community foundations in the Program. The one at Dade Community Foundation, for example, has 50-60 people, made up of partners from the county's largest law firms. They know the basics of charitable law, and Foundation staff educate them on the newest wrinkles, and most importantly, on how they and their clients are well served by a community foundation. Such a committee positions the community foundation to do serious asset development.

While only a handful of participants formed a committee, almost all strive to maintain relations with the key estate attorneys and advisors in town. Sometimes this takes the form of a "take a lawyer to lunch" effort, or a periodic hosted breakfast or luncheon event with such advisors.

Development role #2: Communications vehicles

All participants in the Program used several media for communicating to key constituents, typically prospective and current donors, professional advisors, institutional funders, and program partners. Chief among them:

Brochures. They typically describe "ways of giving" — the different types of funds and philanthropic services offered by a community foundation. The Greater Memphis Community Foundation issues a monthly newsletter for advisors called *Creative Giving.* Each issue features an article written by an expert drawn from its 24-member board of contributors.

Annual reports. They describe the mission and activities of the foundation, the purposes of different funds, the role of key donors, programmatic activities, and financial information. Their emphases and format are often changed. A few participants publish reports every other year.

Newsletters. Appearing two to four times per year, they provide updates to different constituents — donors, nonprofit organizations, and local government — on the variety of ways the community foundation serves their interests.

Press releases. Most participants issue one to three press releases per year announcing new gifts, staff, programs, board members, and projects — much of the same material that may go into newsletters.

Presentations. Staff often make presentations to Chamber of Commerce and Rotary Club meetings, Regional Association of Grantmakers meetings, and other civic groups — as a way to introduce the purposes and roles the community foundation plays.

Annual meetings. Annual meetings are occasions for presenting grant awards, honoring board members or donors, unveiling new programs, and hearing the experience of national experts.

Development role #3: Broaden the base of donors

In the last 20 years, the demographics of most communities have changed dramatically, and they continue to change. This creates a world of new opportunities for community foundations, once their boards, staffs, and advisors determine how they want their institution to serve different segments of its community. With changing demographics comes increased variety in how wealth is created, deployed, saved, and disposed, and how people care for each other through charity, philanthropy, and community building activities.

Community foundations in this Program have kept pace with these changing demographics in some areas of operation more than in others. They've done well in two important areas: forming more diverse advisory committees and creating diversity in their grants lists. But when asked, they give themselves lower marks in diversifying two other areas: board membership and especially, donor base. These trends are interconnected, in that advisory committees tend to influence grantee selection, and boards tend to influence outreach to donors.

Some participants in the Program have responded by creating "minority funds," typically set up with their own advisory group to guide resource development as well as grantmaking activities. African American Funds, Hispanic Funds, and/or Women's Funds have been created in The Dayton Foundation, The Community Foundation of Greater Lorain County, and The Rochester Area Foundation. Such funds are said to serve as a visible vehicle for (1) involving minorities and women in organized philanthropy, with funds accumulated to serve those segments; (2) leadership development for minorities and women, with advancement possibilities to other community foundation committees. Two disadvantages: (1) they tend to require their own staff; (2) they could send a message that the main body of funds held by the community foundation are *not* for the benefit of minorities or women.

Other participants, notably The El Paso Community Foundation and Dade Community Foundation, have chosen *not* to separate minority from majority in their fund structure. Advantages: (1) they broaden the base of ownership in the foundation as a whole through the active inclusion of "minorities" (recognize that in those two communities Anglos are the minority) on foundation-wide committees and activities; (2) they tend not to encounter the two disadvantages cited in the previous paragraph. The main disadvantage: they do not afford the advantages cited in the previous paragraph.

The Arizona Community Foundation, rather than create separate minority funds, created a Social Justice Fund through a lead gift from a minority board member with a strong interest in the issue. Such a fund allows the foundation to focus on a variety of issues affecting a broad spectrum of the community in an inclusive way.

The keys to actively engaging minority communities — as well as "the public at large" — in institutional philanthropy are actively being sought by a number of foundations. Central to El Paso's approach is to make philanthropy "everybody's business," not just those in the 36 percent tax bracket. Publishing its annual report in the Sunday paper is part of that approach, as are its efforts to save everyone's favorite downtown theater from the wrecking ball, attracting thousands of small donations.

The same spirit — broadening the public's interest in philanthropy — motivated the Community Foundation for Southeastern Michigan and Arizona Community Foundation to sponsor Independent Sector's "Give Five" campaign. The campaign — presented in print media and billboards — encourages all persons to give five percent of their income and five percent of their time to causes of their choice.

It also motivated the Community Foundation of Greater Lorain County to hold and manage endowments created by virtually all the school districts in its county; more importantly it coaches school district committee members in the fine art of resource development.

In some communities, growth comes from cultivating less traditional segments: the new arrivals to town, especially to the Sun Belt or other rapidly growing communities; a first generation of community givers, especially those memorializing their histories or families; or those who traditionally give only to their church or college. These segments can be targeted by fund developers, and reached by the foundation's newsletter or in presentations by staff to group luncheons.

Broadening the base of donors at the Greater Triangle Community Foundation (North Carolina) meant "include corporations." When the Leadership Program was first designed, conventional wisdom held that corporations would not give to endowment. But the experience of almost all participants proved otherwise. At Greater Triangle Community Foundation, 52 percent of gifts (by value) to endowment during the match period were from corporations, 31 gifts in all. For the 10 community foundations in Round Two, gifts from corporations made up an average of 17 percent of gifts to endowment.

Development role #4: Donor relations

Donor relations refers to the activities intended to keep existing donors interested in and happy with the "philanthropic services" they receive from the foundation. The full range of communications activities highlighted earlier in this chapter are donor relations activities, since they keep donors informed of the foundation's activities. But those devices are essentially impersonal; they are one-way only and are sent to everyone on the foundation's list.

Two-way communication and custom tailored communication are the kinds of communication that growth-minded directors really want to do, but seldom find the time to do. Sitting down and talking with someone who has already given $5,000, $25,000, or $100,000 allows a director to get to know the donor's real interests and especially how those interests have been sharpened given the rewarding experience of their last gift. Most directors increasingly realize that the relationship between donor and foundation is strengthened through these talks.

The intensive donor relations work that prevailed at most sites while making the match subsided afterwards. But a small number of foundations had not been particularly intense even during the match making period. The Community Foundation Serving Richmond and Central Virginia, for one, had not done anything special to make the match, since it had just successfully concluded a different "campaign" and did not want to start a new one. Instead, it assertively communicated its "message of service" as far and wide as it could, and continued its work with estate attorneys and financial advisors at a level pace all through the five year period.

What convinces donors to give to a community foundation? Many community foundations note that donors actually give "through" a foundation, not "to" it. The distinction is more than semantic. A donor can recommend a specific beneficiary, indicate particular areas of interest, or leave the choice entirely to the discretion of the foundation.

Seen in this light, the community foundation is more of an intermediary than a destination, and as such provides a service to the donor. Not only does the foundation have professional staff that can select the best options for the donor, it also draws on professional investment managers to provide full-time and long-term stewardship to endowment funds.

The following are cited by community foundations as motives for giving, as revealed by donors:

- the opportunity to do something significant for the community;

- the role and philosophy of the foundation in helping to formulate solutions to local problems;

- the ease and usefulness of giving to (or through) the foundation for achieving the donor's charitable goals;

- the recognition donors get as donors;

- the value and security of a gift made to "a savings account" (an endowment) rather than "a checking account" (an annual operating fund drive);

- the specific program initiative created by the foundation, along with its other grantmaking programs;

- the opportunity to be of immediate help in meeting a challenge grant or a campaign goal.

- the tax advantages of contributing to a community foundation, which are superior to creating a private foundation.

Development role #5: Support the board

Board members play a role equally important in the planned giving approach as in the short-term match-raising period. In both, board members, colleagues, clients, and connections are extremely important resources. They create the core entries for two key lists: the list of prospective donors and the list of advisors to prospective donors.

Three very different examples: (1) The Madison Community Foundation's board chair, also an estate attorney, advised a client to include the foundation in her will. The result: a gift of $15 million in permanent, discretionary endowment. (2) The board of the Baltimore Community Foundation, wanting to show its community that it meant to become a major force, raised the entire match from its own membership. (3) Foundation Northwest found itself without the development expertise of its staff director and still several hundred thousand dollars short of its $1 million match requirement. The board undertook to finish the job itself, from making appointments and presentations to follow-up.

Later in the Program, after making the match, the Baltimore Community Foundation received support for its development and marketing proposal from a local philanthropist who wanted to help the foundation expand its base of support. This same approach, in which the community foundation seeks support from a few close individual or institutional stakeholders to support the costs of a development person and activities, is being pursued by the Greater New Orleans Foundation as well, and being considered by a number of others.

Just setting up meetings between prospective donor and board member is an important support staff function. It includes all the associated logistics work: developing lists, conducting background homework on prospects, setting up the meeting(s), ensuring that all written communications pieces are packaged appropriately, writing thank-you notes, and following through in ways that maintain open channels, and so on.

The support work for this development role is similar to the support work needed to staff a professional advisors committee. It typically is more than can be handled by existing support staff, and important enough to warrant a position, especially if the other development roles can be adequately staffed by existing positions.

While conventional wisdom formerly dictated that *all* board members be chosen for their access to wealth, this criterion is outdated. First, resource development functions tend to be concentrated in a development committee of the board, suggesting that people with other strengths can serve in other ways. Second, development committees often reach outside the board to attract members who can be effective liaisons to people of wealth (to a professional advisors committee, for example), suggesting that board membership is no longer a prerequisite for resource development duty. And finally, since a considerable number of gifts to endowment come from people of modest means, board members can be chosen for their connections to people motivated less by tax benefits and more by philanthropy, community service, and other forms of altruism.

Development role #6: Technical specialist

Charitable tax law, estate law, and bank trustee law are sufficiently daunting that few would claim to be expert, yet the fluency in these fields displayed by virtually all executive directors in this Program was remarkable. None of the participants felt the need to hire this expertise, since it was already resident with the executive director. As a foundation grows, it may become necessary to hire a full-time staff member with these skills. We cite two areas of technical specialty as examples, integrating small trusts and private foundations into the community foundation, and servicing "supporting organizations."

An option for people of wealth is to create a supporting organization rather than a private foundation. A supporting organization is treated more favorably by the IRS than a private foundation. This is because it is embedded in a public foundation that is managed with greater representation of the public on its board.

While a supporting organization is incorporated separately from the community foundation, the community foundation is typically given the authority to manage its funds, manage its grantmaking, and be represented on its board. As several participants have discovered, supporting organizations represent a substantial growth opportunity for community foundations.

The Arizona Community Foundation created two new supporting organizations, one for science education ($8 million), the other for hearing-impaired persons ($2 million). The Tucson Community Foundation created an $8 million supporting organization to support work in communications. The Community Foundation for Southeastern Michigan also helped create two supporting organizations, one whose $6 million in resources will become discretionary, and another of $7 million whose resources are already discretionary. Greenville Community Foundation and Greater New Orleans Foundation had supporting organizations nearing fruition.

Many community foundations work to assimilate small trusts into their care by selling their efficiencies as administrators of charitable funds. Banks, under pressure from regulators to be more efficient, often view managing a small trust as a burden, especially if grants are to be disbursed. As a result, typically a bank transfers the resources to the community foundation, which books the resources and makes grants, while the bank manages the resources and collects a fee. Sometimes these funds come with designated purposes, honored by the foundation, but other times those purposes can be broadened, or even made discretionary. As this book went to press, the Community Foundation of Greater Greenville was about to absorb a $5 million private foundation and treat its funds as discretionary.

Development role #7: Create special projects

In making the match, participants learned to use its community initiative — the project undertaken to meet the community leadership goal of the Leadership Program — as a selling point in its approach to donors. Linking program development to resource development worked well, but few participants took advantage of the power of this approach later on. The Tucson Community Foundation, on the other hand, hired a development specialist to design a program in response to a special request. Someone who had watched the foundation grow from afar approached it saying, "Your interest is children and prevention, mine is health and athletics; here's $100,000 to design and start up a program that combines our interest." The implication was that more money was forthcoming if the foundation did a good job with the first gift.

Other participants are contemplating something similar: hiring a person to design projects in response to current or prospective donors' interests.

In some foundations, non-permanent money or so-called "in-and-out money" or "flow-through funds," can be used to create prospects or supplement others. These are funds that are not permanent endowment but can be drawn down for special purposes, usually on advice or recommendation of the donor. Most of the donor-advised funds at The Central New York Community Foundation are of this kind; the principal is used for grantmaking, and the interest earned while the money is under management by the foundation is kept as a management fee. Non-permanent money can be very useful in supporting foundation initiatives. The East Tennessee Foundation has been particularly adept at securing project monies and leveraging them to create permanent endowment.

Results: Growth in commitment and skills

A major result of participation in this Program certainly includes increased discretionary financial resources for all participants. But perhaps more important, especially for the long term, the foundations developed increased *skills* in the resource development arena. These skills, in turn, came after both board and staff committed themselves to putting the community foundation on a fast track to growth.

These are not soft items or intangibles that count less than hard money. "Commitment, resources, and skills" are what define "capacity." They are both the route to capacity building efforts and their outcome.

On the next page is an itemization of "capacities gained" — in addition to greater fund balances — as a result of participants' resource development activities. Obviously, these didn't happen equally at each foundation, just as increases in fund balances were not uniform. They do, however, comprise both a list of outcomes of their most recent stage of growth and inputs to the next stage. As such, they also make a convenient checklist that other resource developing institutions can use to assess their current capacities.

Commitment: Commitment by board and staff . . .

- To learn how financial growth happens and what it requires;

- To take the institution "to the next level," however defined;

- To put in place, through some expenditure, the infrastructure needed to take the foundation to the next level.

Resources: Resources of the *non*-financial kind, including . . .

- Persuasive story lines or cases to help potential donors distinguish the community foundation from other options for giving, for partnership, and for support;

- A variety of communication vehicles for telling the foundation story to a variety of audiences;

- Links to newspaper, radio and TV media that know how to cover the activities of the foundation and its community partners, beneficiaries, and benefactors;

- On-going relationships with professional advisors (estate attorneys, CPAs, etc.) in which they learn about the virtues of a community foundation as both a short-term and long-term resource, and in which the community foundation is moved closer to prospective short-term and long-term donors;

- Mailing lists (updated and computer-friendly) that increasingly include such valued community segments as: major law, financial advisory, and accounting firms; traditionally-defined people of wealth, new wealth and recently arrived wealth; traditionally-defined community leaders, nontraditionally-defined and future community leaders; past and current contributors; nonprofit and voluntary organizations; corporate leadership.

Skills: Skill in those practices that . . .

- Deliberately seek to broaden the base of donors, including reconnoitering and prospecting, identifying credible appeals and finding credible links to new prospects and learning of their interests;

- Help current donors increase their involvement and commitment to the community foundation, including providing opportunities for donors to learn more about both the spirit and the technique of philanthropic giving, and about specific opportunities that touch their interests;

- Skill in the legal forms of transferring resources into the community foundation, from individuals and their estates, from private and public corporations, and from the myriad old and new forms of trusts.

Chapter Four

Taking on Capacity: **Organizational Commitment**

In this chapter we continue our presentation of findings and lessons, focusing on the second ingredient of capacity — commitment. We describe several manifestations of commitment, beginning with board leadership, growth by plan, and diversification. We then discuss how participants in Leadership Program developed sources of support for operations — a "growth budget." Finally we describe the administrative skills required, particularly in human resource management, to keep pace with a growing organization, and the types of assistance executive directors sought to implement change.

Organizational commitment: A key ingredient of capacity

All organizations involve work. The purpose of any organization is to undertake work that cannot be done by individuals acting alone. The specific work to be done is usually suggested in the name of the group or in its mission statement.

Doing any kind of work well, whether alone or organized, usually leads to invitations or opportunities to do more. In turn this leads to getting more people involved, which usually leads to dividing up the work along lines that allegedly contribute to the organization's effectiveness. A leader or governing body coordinates or supervises, resulting in guidelines or policies to give structure to activities, avoid confusion, and keep the organization moving toward its goals.

It takes commitment to make organizations grow. It takes other things as well, notably resources and skills. But without commitment to the principles of work organization, resources are more likely to flow *through* the organization rather than mold to a growing and sustainable infrastructure. Resources are like nutrients, meant to help the organization "bulk up." An organization growing in capacity is one that skillfully uses resources to help it bulk up; an organization not growing in capacity is one that merely consumes resources.

For these basic reasons, a commitment to strong organizational infrastructure is a part of the capacity picture, for without it, work is misdirected and scattered, and people are isolated rather than connected. While the Leadership Program was designed to help community foundations develop their discretionary financial resources as well as their community leadership skills, the *strengthening* of the organization itself resulted in interconnected, not coincidental ways that went well beyond the original two goals.

Organizational growth meant growing pains

Working toward the two major goals of the Program — growth in financial resources and in community leadership — had a synergistic effect. Progress in one helped progress in the other. The synergistic effect worked this way. First, most community foundations typically added staff for their community initiative. Since the executive director had been the primary staff person for most programmatic efforts, this addition freed the executive director to develop financial resources and expand the foundation's typical role in the community.

When financial resources grew from the foundation's endowment building efforts, the existing financial and investment management procedures became stressed, leading to additional financial management staff, computerization, new administrative routines, and support staff. As staff were added, the entire human resource function grew, and executive directors added personnel administration to their job.

On the programming side, as the foundations demonstrated community leadership skills, they became more visible throughout their communities and were invited to do even more. As they were invited to do more, they stretched in those directions — and grew some more, if they could.

This phase, of being overloaded, peaked for most participants in the third or fourth year, part of the re-grouping period after making the match (see Chapter Three). A period of "taking stock" occurred in which plans for taking the community foundation to the next level were formulated. For the most part, growth led to more growth.

But growth led also to growing pains. Adding a new staff person to a three-person office is not easy, especially if that new person is more highly qualified than the people already there, or if that person comes from a very different background.

To ward off confusion or charges of unfairness — from inside the organization and outside — participants developed guidelines and policies. For example, personnel policies clarified the rules governing compensation, perks, and authority. Grantmaking guidelines were used to communicate the purposes of the foundation's discretionary funds to the larger nonprofit and foundation communities.

Results: Organizational commitment

Several areas of organization infrastructure became more developed as a result of commitments made to growth and to the momentum created by growth in financial resources and programming activity. These include board leadership, growth by design, and greater diversity.

Board leadership

Board leadership was crucial to the growth of virtually all participating community foundations. It was one of the single most important ingredients in the emergence of these foundations, since it is at the board level that a commitment to grow is made and institutionalized.

Board members contributed to the growth of their community foundations in these ways:

- They directly aided fund development efforts to make the required $1 million match by pooling their knowledge on likely prospects to approach, enlisting staff to "do the ask," and adding their prestige and influence to the overall effort.

- They gave increasingly of their time and energy — to the growing role and influence of the community foundation, typically placing the community foundation higher on their own list of voluntary activities. Many spent considerable time learning the intricacies of the community foundation field, going to conferences and workshops, as well as reading the literature.

- They contributed substantially to the development of plans and policies — the tools of governance — that served to guide the growth as well as the stability of the foundation. Typically, these covered investment management, human resource administration, grantmaking priorities and guidelines, eligibility guidelines for new funds, and overall direction.

- They helped raise some of the resources needed for the annual administrative budget. Many helped broker in-kind donations (equipment, furniture, skills) or provided offices or professional services at well below market rates.

- New board members helped the foundation connect to new constituencies, broadening the base of governance and perspective.

- They helped advance the community initiative, although largely playing a background role. Their greatest role was in helping the foundation choose a suitable initiative from among competing alternatives, adding perspective as to how it would play in their community. Especially interested board members served on the initiative's advisory committee.

- They helped their foundation become more sophisticated in governance and management. Divisions of labor appeared at the board level, shifting first from a committee of the whole to operating with an executive committee and separate committees for distribution (or grants), special projects or programs, development, and investment/finance. Because of the increasing demands on their time (and staff time) brought on by growth, boards shifted from do-everything boards to policy boards, increasingly delegating authority to staff as expressed in written policies. They concurred less routinely with staff, and increasingly set the foundation's direction itself. The rate of this evolution varied considerably, with some foundations already at this point at the time of entry into the Program.

By the time most participants were accepted into the Leadership Program, and certainly by the time they had finished, they had boards comparable to the hospital, the symphony, the United Way, the Chamber of Commerce, and perhaps even the university.

Rapid growth only added to this prestige. And since most boards genuinely sought the membership of minorities, and since most foundations were increasingly active in non-traditional segments of the community, the community foundation board became a more attractive alternative for minority leadership to join.

Board members with long-term involvement but no current history of contributions were encouraged to rotate off the board, allowing new members to come on. This was difficult to do, given the often significant contribution of founding board members, but accomplished with aplomb.

Growth plan

There are many ways for an organization *not* to grow in size or usefulness. Since one can sputter and stall even more easily than grow, creating and using a plan to guide growth was found necessary by virtually all participants.

For most participants, three different planning periods occurred during their life with the Leadership Program. The first period actually began *before* participants were chosen, at the time Ford's program announcement inviting applications came out. Some foundations had recently completed a planning process as an intentional part of their growth; others realized that to compete successfully for inclusion in the Program, they'd need to put their most capable face forward. In either case, the sponsor's group of advisors that read applications and visited sites were quick to notice, as they were directed, whether the organization "had its act together," i.e., had the capacity to build more capacity.

Having gone through a recent planning process, as well as writing and speaking knowledgeably from a plan, definitely helped foundation spokespeople give that impression. Foundations chosen for the Program were those with a knack for demonstrating that they knew what they wanted and knew how to get there.

The second period involved a board and staff decision on a plan of action for raising the required $1 million in new permanent discretionary or broad field-of-interest funds. Usually a specific plan of action — rather than a broad strategic plan — required board members to present a polished definition of their organization. Given the complexities of a community foundation, this was not an easy task. The alternative was to smoothly hand off these development discussions to the executive director.

The third period followed the success of making the match when foundations were confronted with the basic dilemma of growth: "there's more work to be done, and the community wants more from us, so how can we respond without having to spend more on overhead?" This led to plenty of organizational hand-wringing: "Are we supposed to get bigger? Is overhead unthinkable? Do we *always* have to raise funds? Is the future certain?"

By this time, typically late into Years Four and Five of participation, many of the organizational habits which define a culture of growth — particularly intentionality, fortitude, and moving towards opportunity — had time to set. A majority of board/staff combinations were eager for more. Some remained unfocused or weary. A few were downright wary of growth, or at least of the effort, challenge, and risk demanded. This third planning period involved more ambivalence and less urgency than the first two, which led to spottier implementation of growth plans.

Planning isn't everything, and considerable growth can and did result simply from the momentum put in place earlier. Many had learned that even substantial departures from their plan to make the match had little ill effect. But this learning may not always serve well. Where growth has happened with a few substantial gifts rather than through sustained attention to growth-inducing activities, there may be risk of spindly rather than sturdy infrastructure.

In short, most participants learned how to grow — in financial resources, stature, leadership, and organizational infrastructure. How they have used that learning to create permanent habits or reliable guidance is what varies from place to place.

Diversifying the organization

Growth and activity preceded pressure to open up the foundation's operation to more participation from more diverse elements of the community.

Most participants eventually recognized that the initial set of board members would not serve them indefinitely and that changes would have to be made. The board got the foundation off the ground, or helped position it to take advantage of a major opportunity such as this Leadership Program presented.

When participants genuinely thought of themselves as "growing," they knew the board would have to grow in new ways as well — especially in terms of outreach to new constituencies. Sometimes "new constituencies" meant new wealth that resulted from the mergers, acquisitions, and buyouts of the boom 1980s, or new wealth that had followed the sun to the fast-growth communities of the southeast and southwest. Sometimes it meant outreach to new ethnic arrivals, especially to Hispanic and Asian cultures, or to older ethnic communities, especially African American.

Some of the pressure to change the board's composition came from the Ford Foundation itself, which has an assertive policy calling for diversified board and staff within its own institution, and among all its grantees — in terms of race and gender. This theme was reinforced at the annual meetings of Program participants, in which participants discussed the problems and opportunities of diversification. It also was reinforced in Rainbow Research's annual survey of participating community foundations that asked for the diversity profile of board, staff, and committees.

Efforts by participants to diversify have borne fruit in some areas of operation more than others. Diversifying the grants list proved easiest, as did diversifying advisory committees. Diversifying staff and board was the hardest. As noted in Chapter Three, diversifying the donor base has only begun, and only in a few places.

Female representation on boards grew from 22 percent to 29 percent, and minority representation from 15 percent to 22 percent — across all eight participants in Round One. For Round Two, with only four years to report, female representation grew from 30 percent to 32 percent, and minority representation grew from 11 percent to 14 percent — among 10 participants.

For Round One, the percentage of professional staff that were female began at 70 percent and shrank to 60 percent. The minority percentage grew from 11 percent to 16 percent, for the eight Round One participants. For Round Two, the percentage of female professional staff began at 82.5 percent and shrank to 72 percent in four years. The percentage that were minority shrank from 16.5 percent to 11 percent. Realize that small numbers are involved in these analyses.

Expanding the foundation's ownership and operation to more diverse interests has not been easy. Many foundations report frustration, internal resistance, and even setbacks. Some foundations feel

that increased diversity on the board comes at the expense of financial resource development efforts. Some claim that qualified
minority board members are hard to find or that their participation
is minimal.

A few foundations have had the opposite experience. Those with
a commitment to diversity have successfully recruited minority
board members. "Where board members were chosen originally
almost entirely for their financial resource development clout," according to one executive director, "choices are now guided more
by their outreach to new constituencies."

Other executives acknowledge there need not be a trade-off;
many new board members represent new constituencies *and*
access to financial resources. See also pages 71 and 72 regarding
the board's role in development.

Increased diversity at the board level has been achieved by:

Adding flexibility to the board appointment process. Since
board membership changes slowly through attrition, some foundations changed the rules. This included written rules concerning
the number of positions on the board, the term of office, and the
prescribed number of consecutive terms. In many cases, the
"rules" that were changed were unwritten and often unspoken.

*Actively seeking diversity on committees that do not require
board membership.* In many places these include project advisory committees, the distribution committee, and the investment
committee.

Actively seeking diversity in the donor base. This has taken
the form of marketing named family funds, donor advised funds,
minority funds, and memorial funds. Interested or significant
donors can often make good board members.

Actively scouting likely organizations. Consulting esteemed
minorities for their suggestions, and scouting out organizations
known to have higher minority representations, such as service or-

ganizations, business associations, church groups, neighborhood associations, and professional groups is a tactic that has brought new stakeholders to these community foundations.

Results: Financial resources

Funding growth: Sources of administrative money

All organizations — large and small, public, private, and nonprofit are faced with the task of funding their administration. Although finding funds for their programs and projects present a difficult enough task, it's funding the overhead — the cost of doing business — that is the biggest financial challenge.

Different kinds of organizations have found ways to do this, with inventiveness as the key. Community foundations, by their nature, present some unique opportunities for creative financing, as revealed in the analysis of Table 4-1.

Table 4-1 shows the "average" budget, on both the revenue side and expense side, for the eight participants in Round One, the ten in Round Two and the nine in Round Three, and an average calculated for all 27 participants. These budgets were in effect on January 1, 1992, just as Round One ended, Round Two ended its third year, and Round Three ended its first year. The total funds managed by these foundations are quite different on the average (shown on the bottom line), given the two-year difference in starting dates from one Round to the next. The figure given for total funds at the bottom of Table 4-1 includes both permanent and non-permanent funds (the one place in this book both are shown), because it costs to administer both types, and that cost is typically reflected in administrative budgets on both the revenue and expense side.

Table 4 - 1
Administrative Revenue & Expenses for Participants in
Rounds One, Two and Three *(January 1, 1992)*

	Round One		Round Two		Round Three		Total	
Revenue	$ Average	%	$ Average	%	$ Average	%	$ Average	%
Administrative Endowment	22,800	4	10,709	3	25,108	11	19,091	5
Administrative Fees	213,457	38	112,357	32	75,012	33	129,864	34
Investment Income	70,616	12	24,720	7	13,075	6	34,437	9
Float	49,633	9	18,044	5	22,161	10	28,776	8
Fee for Service	4,625	1	4,320	1	5,219	2	4,710	1
Individual Gifts	63,153	11	30,214	9	18,013	8	35,907	10
Corporate Gifts	22,838	4	12,000	3	6,667	3	13,433	4
Foundation Gifts	7,500	1	33,855	10	28,877	13	24,387	7
Grants to Operate Programs	40,504	7	49,508	14	28,586	12	39,866	11
Other	70,921	13	51,410	15	8,038	3	42,734	11
Total Revenue	**$ 566,047**	**100**	**$ 347,138**	**99**	**$ 230,757**	**101**	**$ 373,206**	**100**

Expenses	$ Average	%	$ Average	%	$ Average	%	$ Average	%
Staff	316,560	60	203,177	60	136,262	60	214,467	60
Office	79,649	15	38,803	11	29,411	13	47,775	13
Equipment	6,128	1	9,995	3	4,174	2	6,909	2
Public Relations	38,178	7	28,121	8	18,225	8	27,802	8
Travel, Dues	24,138	5	11,819	3	9,998	4	14,862	4
Accounting, Legal	28,598	5	13,751	4	11,016	5	17,328	5
Other	34,940	7	34,744	10	17,959	8	29,207	8
Total Expenses	**$ 528,191**	**100**	**$ 340,409**	**99**	**$ 227,045**	**100**	**$ 358,260**	**100**

Fund Balance	$ Average	$ Average	$ Average	$ Average
Total	**$ 28,693,965**	**$ 15,776,800**	**$ 8,123,396**	**$ 17,531,377**

91

In this section, we focus on *sources* of administrative revenue. Where does administrative money come from?

Remember that because all figures are averages, they obscure variation. Not shown, then, is the reality that each foundation funds its operations very differently. Some rely primarily on fees, others rely far more on gifts, and a few have very diversified bases of funding. The average profiles for all three Rounds look remarkably similar — remarkable because the size of the foundation (reflected in Total Fund Balance) varies so much from Round to Round, on the average.

The proportion of revenues coming from administrative fees, the Table shows, is similar for a $29 million foundation, a $16 million foundation, and an $8 million foundation, on average. The same can be said for the other sources of revenue. The average expense profile is perhaps even more stable from Round to Round.

This contradicts a finding reported earlier, in *CF/Findings from the Leadership Program for Community Foundations*. In an article entitled "Where Does Administrative Money Come From?" *(Rainbow Research, 1990)*, an analysis of Round One and Two participants showed that larger foundations ($10 million or more) drew more of its administrative revenue from internal sources (the first four lines of the revenue budget shown in Table 4-1), than did smaller foundations, which relied more on support from the outside. The analysis reported here, with more range in foundation size and a larger sample, found no such distinction between smaller and larger foundations.

What are the major sources of administrative money? All but 11 percent of their revenue comes from seven types of sources.

Administrative fees. Fees charged against the foundation's funds typically account for 34 percent of these administrative budgets. But how these fees are charged varies tremendously from place to place. Some foundations charge fees against a fund's income while others charge against its current market value. Some types of funds (donor-advised, for example, which requires more hands-on servicing) are charged more than others. Several foundations charge a lower rate to agency endowments that they manage. Charges are typically set after reviewing the practices of competitive institutions.

Gifts. Gifts to the foundation not earmarked for grantmaking or endowment make up an average of 21 percent of all administrative budgets, irrespective of source. The prevalence of corporate gifts over individual gifts over foundation gifts varies hugely, depending mainly on the fundraising styles of the foundation. Gifts from individuals run high when the foundation sponsors fundraising events or semi-public appeals for support. Some foundations avoid such events or appeals, preferring to appeal to local foundations and corporations.

Grants to operate programs. Many community foundations succeed in securing grant money from other foundations or from local government; ideally these include support for administrative costs. Leadership Program participants could use up to $50,000 of their annual $100,000 grant from the Program to operate their leadership initiatives; the remainder went out in grants. In most cases, such grant monies are placed in their administrative budgets, though sometimes they were allocated to separate program budgets.

Investment income. The interest earned on "idle" administrative funds is a form of investment income that can be spent for operations. In other words, that portion of the administrative budget that is in hand *before* it's actually needed can be put in an interest-bearing checking account or cash instrument, with the interest earned credited to the administrative budget. The earlier in the fiscal year that budget monies are in hand means the larger this source of income can be. At a handful of foundations in this Program, donor-advised funds are received in "non-permanent" rather than "permanent" form. From these funds the foundation gradually pays out the principal in grants, and uses the earnings to pay for administration. This type of earnings is also considered "investment income."

Float. "Float" refers to the yield gained from the temporary use of money on its way, typically, from an internal fund to a grantee. A special case of investment income, it is also known as "income on income" or "interest on interest." It works like this. During one quarter, the Jones Fund earns $500 that is earmarked for disbursement. But before the funds are disbursed they earn interest in a special disbursement account. That practice is called "float" and, as is the practice in many large financial institutions, the money is used to fund administration.

Administrative endowments. Nine of the eighteen participants in Rounds One and Two, and all nine in Round Three have created an "administrative endowment," earnings which are used exclusively to support the administration of the community foundation. Together they constitute an average of five percent of revenues. Raising money for an administrative endowment turned out to be less difficult than anticipated. Depositing discretionary gifts into an administrative endowment is permissible, since it is used for charitable purposes in fulfillment of the foundation's mission. Earnings taken at the beginning of the budget year and deposited in the administrative budget's account earn investment income, until used.

Fees for service. Eight of the twenty-seven foundations in the Program are able to supplement their income by charging fees for certain services they provide. This typically includes charges for performing fiscal agent services; and for providing staff or consultation service to private foundations, corporate foundations, or regional associations of grantmakers. While providing an average of only one percent of revenues, many would like to build on this infrequently used option. Broadly speaking, the source of revenue called "administrative fees" is also a fee for service — a fee charged for servicing charitable accounts, a major business of community foundations.

Other. "Other" has two distinguishable sources, plus a still indistinguishable "other." One part is "rental income," typically from a building the foundation owns. The other is "carry-over from the previous year," more of a cash-flow consideration than a genuine source of revenue.

Funding growth takes money, and money to support growth is difficult to come by. The above analysis shows that such money comes from inside *and* outside the foundation. From outside, growth is supported by undesignated gifts to the foundation, by grants to support operations, and by grants that support program-matic activity. It's this last source that is typically the largest, at least among rapidly growing community foundations, and not always easy to replace. Program grants are typically quite limited in duration. This Leadership Program, after five years, has pro-vided the longest period of support of any programs offered to community foundations. But when the money runs out, it's hard to replace.

Finding that replacement money is often the source of high anxi-ety, and not just for the program person who may have been supported during the five years. Typically there's more than a po-sition on the line, there's an entire set of relationships with key segments of the community that have been developed to support the program. Those relationships are placed at risk if replacement money is not found.

Fortunately, most rapidly growing foundations have learned to attract money from outside that allows them to conduct potentially useful and visible programs for their communities. As the larger funding community began to see what foundations could do — and showing off the leadership initiative was the major vehicle for showing them — it responded with additional opportunities to ex-ercise their skills and play a leadership role. Typically the program officer hired with Leadership money has had her or his job ex-panded to include staffing other initiatives, as well as managing the discretionary grantmaking cycles and donor advised funds.

In general, grants for programs are an unstable source of income. When there are grants from several sources, each with its own beginning and ending dates, the overall flow of revenues into the administrative budget becomes uneven. The challenge to the foundation is two-fold: to manage revenues to provide an even, predictable flow; and to build up the permanent, chargeable financial resource base to offset reliance on irregular income. Ideally the visibility and reputation gained from operating successful grant-making programs is parlayed into the development of permanent financial resources.

A program costing $100,000 to operate requires at least $10,000,000 in chargeable financial resources, assuming the foundation charges a one percent administrative fee on those financial resources (and assuming, to simplify discussion, no investment income). And if the foundation is growing rapidly and the administrative budget doubles during that period, perhaps $20,000,000 is really needed to sustain the foundation's *rate* of growth.

The most reliable source of administrative funds is fees charged against the funds managed by the foundation. The larger these funds, the greater the fees collected, and the more money available for administering the organization. Charging fees and collecting interest from funds under one's own control is as close as one can get to "administrative self-sufficiency."

But self-sufficiency is an illusory goal; no foundation comes close to attaining it, regardless of size. A recent study by the Council on Foundations (1989) showed that even the largest community foundations in the country are able to fund no more than 57 percent of their operations from fees, a level approximated by only three of the larger foundations in this Program.

Without sufficient new chargeable financial resources, the foundation must work to attract additional program dollars or provide additional services to its publics, for a fee. This works to the extent that public and private institutions and new donors are willing to invest in foundations as vehicles or partners for their own local charitable interests. Many such institutions *are* increasingly willing.

"It takes money to make money"

Growth costs. It's a principle widely recognized in entrepreneurial circles, but one that has not been discussed widely in the non-profit sector, including community foundations.

Instead the conventional wisdom among community foundations is that the way to grow is to develop chargeable funds. But developing chargeable funds is only part of the picture. Another part, seen more clearly through the experience of the Leadership Program for Community Foundations, is that growth requires a commitment of administrative dollars, as well. In other words, it takes money to make money.

The Leadership Program provided participants with up to $50,000 per year that they could use to support their community initiative and fund development activities. During site visits in the first two years of the Program, participants were seen to have expanded their offices, added staff, re-designed their brochures, hosted receptions, and spent time learning from their peers.

How does spending administrative dollars lead to chargeable financial resources? Money spent on financial resource development stands a better chance of repayment than if spent in other ways. Money spent on projects that can showcase the foundation and its abilities can be repaid if communicated in ways that support financial resource development efforts.

One can see in the lower portion of Table 4-1 the items that growing community foundations are spending their money on.

Staff. Staff is the big ticket item, in community foundations as elsewhere, accounting for an average of 60 percent of expenses. Some of this budget growth from smaller to larger foundations reflects salary raises, but most of it reflects the addition of new staff. (Remember that on January 1, 1992, Round One participants were substantially bigger in total funds than Round Two participants which were substantially bigger than Round Three.) Growth in compensation clearly parallels the growth of the entire administrative budget. Some of the growth in compensation reflects the fact that previously volunteered or donated services became paid services, such as the audit, secretarial, bookkeeping, or legal services. Some of it reflects growth in benefits. Many staff, particularly executive directors, previously relied on their spouse's health insurance and other benefits — including salary — during the early lean years of these community foundations.

Adding program staff early in the life of a small community foundation has the beneficial effect of freeing up the executive's time to pursue financial resource development. It gives the community an indication of what a foundation can do with discretionary money. This has been one of the biggest lessons of the entire Leadership Program.

Office expenses. Office expenses were the next largest budget gainer. This may seem mundane at first, but it includes important keys to growth: stationery, postage, supplies, and the telephone. Why would such items go up in expense? It's because these community foundations are communicating more, creating brochures, newsletters, and annual reports to get the word out to larger and larger mailing lists. Foundations are reaching deeper and wider into key segments of the communities that will help them grow.

Rent also increased. The offices of fast growth foundations can usually be recognized in three ways. First, they become increasingly separated from their parent or sheltering organizations — typically the United Way, a bank, Chamber of Commerce, or Junior League.

Second, their location and look announce that "this is the home of a permanent endowment." Basement offices with lots of cardboard boxes do not, it was recognized, offer the look of perpetuity that prospective donors have a right to expect.

Third, freshly hung drywall abounds, as the community foundation breaks through walls to occupy adjoining offices. Six of the eight community foundations in Round One expanded their offices during their first year with the Program, and the two others soon after.

Public relations. Public relations expenses grew in tandem with office expenses. They include printing, promotions, communications and public relations consultants. This category of expense supports improved annual reports, improved donor materials, and improved brochures describing different aspects of community foundation activities.

Launching the $1 million match drive required of Leadership Program participants was the occasion for dressing up their promotional materials. Most had been revised two to three years previously. Now there were more funds to spend on design consultants and more attractive graphics, and larger print runs to expanded mailing lists — coupled with a more impressive story to tell that comes with stronger grantmaking and donor services.

Accounting and legal. Expenses for accounting, audit, and legal services increased partly because there was more activity from year to year. Legal papers for a greater variety of donor services had to be created, and they increased because some services shifted from volunteer to paid positions. Bookkeeping and accounting practices became increasingly more complex.

Legal and accounting firms often donate services to young community foundations operating on a shoestring. This is motivated by charity, as well as an interest in showing influential board members what they can do. But after a few years of steady growth, the community foundation can expect to pay for this service.

Travel and dues. Travel and membership dues also go together among the high growth budget lines. They reflect a commitment by these foundations to professional education, primarily conferences of the Council on Foundations. These meetings, the Fall Workshop for Community Foundations, as well as the Annual Meeting which includes private, corporate, and operating foundations, have proven to be valuable — both through the formal sessions and the informal opportunities to network with colleagues from elsewhere. Program officers increasingly have also been able, through increases in this budget line, to attend conferences related to the issue areas they are developing. Board members find the Council meetings helpful in discovering how their counterparts operate.

Equipment. Equipment growth, for the most part, reflects the purchase of computers, software, and related furniture and accessories — items that no organization can afford to be without. They significantly increase the capacity of the community foundation. Their major duties are word processing, bookkeeping, fund accounting, donor and prospect tracking, grants tracking, bulk mailings, and desktop publishing of newsletters.

An interesting sidelight: the introduction of office computers with donor tracking and fund tracking software has rapidly changed the staffing pattern of the smallest community foundations. Many of these tasks, formerly done by the first bookkeeper/grants administrator, can now be handled easily by computer.

In conclusion, it appears that a community foundation that wants to grow can strategically design its administrative budget to aid that growth. The growth of small community foundations can be aided and accelerated by investments in operating capacity — staff, communications, board and staff development, and office computers in particular.

How one spends administrative money can directly affect the immediate prospects of growth. Growth requires a commitment to grow, expressed with an administrative budget that supports it. The board of a growing community foundation needs to recognize that the administrative budget is not merely the "operating" budget — it's actually the "growth" budget.

Financial and investment management

During the first two years of the Leadership Program, the attention of board and staff was focused primarily on financial resource development, the community initiative, and managing growth.

But after securing $1 million in new money, executive directors and boards turned much of their attention inward — to financial management. After getting the attention of the public and the professional advisor community, they needed to assure themselves that they could responsibly and cost-effectively manage large sums of money entrusted to them in perpetuity.

Financial management practices changed with growth, corresponding to the introduction of office computers in even the smallest offices. Investment management practices changed as well. In the earliest days of the community foundation, when the usual financial resource development strategy meant that board members asked their friends and colleagues for contributions, the board took responsibility for investment management upon itself.

But with growth, two trends became evident: (a) a move from volunteer to professional management; (b) more formalized investment policies, allowing more tolerance for risk.

Professional management. When Round One participants began the Program on January 1, 1987 (with total financial resources averaging $11.7 million), the top finance person was typically a bookkeeper, and the audit was donated by an accounting firm. Five years later, with total financial resources averaging $28.7 million, all but the smallest of the Round One foundations had a vice president for finance who held an MBA or CPA. This person was at a par with the vice president for programming, and usually with a larger staff complement.

Accounting is now computerized and done internally. Audits are no longer donated by a nearby accounting firm that is waiting solicitously for the foundation to grow. Auditors' and management consultants' advice was sought to establish the kind of controls needed to show credible stewardship. Computers, scarce at the beginning, are now plentiful.

Producing easily auditable financial reports is no longer a problem. All participants still wrestle with the challenge of producing individualized reports to active donors showing their fund balance, earnings, and payouts — especially when their funds have been allocated to multiple money managers.

Increased emphasis on financial management has required major investments of time and money for rapidly growing foundations. "Growth has been so rapid," said one executive director, "that we've been growing out of systems every two years. We've been through more growth than we've digested. The back office — accounting, investment monitoring, grants management — has never caught up. Even so, there's no question that we can't answer within 48 hours."

As these foundations grew while their boards took on additional responsibilities — and as the sense of risk from an uncertain economy increased — there was added pressure to move from volunteer to professional management of funds. The October 1987 crash of the equity market (Round One began in January 1987) further raised the importance of sound and enforceable investment policies.

Several participants recruited a volunteer investment committee of advisors to monitor the foundation's investments. Others used a board committee to monitor the performance of professional managers engaged by the foundation.

A few foundations encouraged competition among different banks or investment firms (even when they were represented on the board); others discouraged it and preferred to use one investment manager.

Formalized policies. Almost all participants have formulated a written strategy intended to strike the optimal balance between growth potential and risk aversion. "Optimal balance," however, was defined differently at most sites, ranging from 20 percent maximum equity participation to as much as 80 percent. "Good stewardship in the name of community requires growth," was often heard as justification for a liberal interpretation of the so-called "prudent man rule." The equities market did not fare well in 1989-90, and the income statements of most of these founda-tions reflect diminished earnings, and in half the cases, losses.

A number of factors combined to make this group of community foundations particularly assertive in articulating and approving written investment guidelines:

- An appetite for discretionary grantmaking;

- The wish to capitalize on bull markets;

- The wish to avoid the damage from the mini-crash of 1987;

- The frequent recourse to a theme of "competent stewardship and money management" in soliciting donations to endowment;

- The wish to replace "pass-through" money that temporarily supports projects with permanent chargeable financial resources;

- The wish to use professionally managed assets as a selling point with donors.

Although no two investment policies are alike, creating them was relatively easy. Implementing them, on the other hand, required substantial political and diplomatic skill. This situation exists be-cause foundation board members are often associated with invest-ment management firms or, in the case of trust form foundations, with banks.

Results: Administrative skills

The evolution of staffing

With growth comes the addition of staff, and with staff often comes additional growth opportunities.

The smallest foundations began this Program with a full-time executive director and a full-time administrative assistant, and perhaps a part-time or off-budget program officer supported by "flow-through" monies. The next stage of evolution included a bookkeeper or a grants assistant to manage the grantmaking paperwork. With growth came a program officer, and perhaps a second officer and/or administrative support for either the fiscal or program side. The largest participants began this Program with such a staff complement.

Securing a full-time program officer was typically the first staff acquisition, and it proved to be a critical step in the lives of Program participants. It allowed the executive director more time for financial resource development activities, particularly in satisfying the match requirement of the Program; more time for the political work needed to position the foundation better; and more time for managing the development of organizational infrastructure.

This advance demanded more from financial management. The next staff person put in place the systems to manage a more complex set of books and track investments, and reported to donors and other groups, as well as the board. This person was often the resident computer expert who purchased hardware and installed software.

More help with financial resource development followed, with one person typically taking on roles as communications specialist, development specialist, and/or donor relations specialist.

Each step meant the executive director became increasingly removed from the day-to-day aspects of these functions. The executive director had to learn to get things done *through* other people.

While the community leadership initiative gave the foundation increasing local renown, the finance and development functions had the largest growth in terms of staff. The so-called "back room operations" — bookkeeping, accounting/control, monitoring funds, and reporting to donors and oversight committees — are labor-intensive as well as computer-imperative.

Table 4-2 reflects the growth in average staff full-time equivalents (FTE) for the three rounds of participants.

Table 4-2
Growth in Average Staff Size (Full-Time Equivalents)

	1987	1988	1989	1990	1991	1992
Round 1	5.0	5.5	6.5	7.0	8.0	9.0
Round 2			3.4	4.5	5.0	5.5
Round 3					2.8	3.4

Human resource management

"If you got our colleagues together in a room, speaking confidentially, they'd say personnel was their biggest bugaboo," said one executive director. "Pay equity is a big problem, especially when someone's been there awhile and a hot shot is then brought in."

That happened often. A "grants assistant" may have been adequate when most grantmaking was done with donor-advised or designated funds. But with programmatic initiatives requiring discretion in the use of discretionary funds, a higher level "project officer" or "program officer" is needed. This person is often a specialist in a particular subject area or a generalist with public and community affairs experience, a skilled group process facilitator, or a person influential in the community affected by the initiative. Bringing such a person on staff necessitated revisiting more than one foundation's entire pay scale, which had been patched together in the days when the foundation was still thinking small.

On the financial side, a really good bookkeeper could manage the books of a $4 to $7 million community foundation, but not much more. When someone with better accounting skills was brought in who could also supervise the bookkeeper, awkwardness and hard feelings resulted. A $20 million foundation can hire someone with comptroller experience, but even this can be inadequate for a $40 million foundation. Most participants outgrew the finance person they had at the beginning of the Program. Financial staff often cost more than program staff, which can also lead to wrinkles in the salary structure as well as peoples' feelings.

No longer is the executive director the chief cook and bottle washer. Executive directors were forced to become personnel administrators, devoting far more time to issues of hiring and training, salaries and benefits, and work group relations. That's because with growth, the key functions of a community foundation — program, development, finance, and administration — become so substantial that the initial division of labor had to change and change again; and change is hard to manage.

Some executive directors learned about supervision painfully, after departures by staffers who could not or would not adapt to the faster pace and oftentimes less organized (and sometimes more organized) style of the community foundation. Executive directors at these foundations acknowledge that they might not have been fully prepared to manage other people. In response, the successful ones studied the personnel policies of more experienced foundations and took leadership classes themselves. They developed better orientation practices for new employees, better benefit packages, better internal communications, and better performance review procedures.

Staff salaries grew as financial resource levels grew. Benefits increased as well, but they achieve professional levels more slowly than salaries. For example, it's a rare participant that has a pension plan. Issues of fair compensation aren't the only areas stretching the administrative skills of the executive director. Problems vary: confused or contradictory supervisory practices, poor job definition or orientation to the position, and unrealistic expectations.

Bringing on a new staff person is time-consuming and difficult for those new to the task. Not all new hires "take," whether due to a confusing job definition or inconsistent supervision. Further, many of these small community foundations pride themselves on their intimate family feeling. Taking on the trappings of a larger, possibly more bureaucratic organization is stressful, even when the need is warranted. Directors of small but growing foundations have learned volumes about recruiting, interviewing, and training a new staff person.

Managing a "diverse" staff has also posed challenges. The Leadership Program has stressed from the beginning that diversity in the community foundation's ownership and operation is the hallmark of a genuine community leadership institution. But some participants have had minority staff leave after just a few weeks or months. Working successfully with minority staff "seems to require a commitment to open up personally, not just organizationally, to more diverse experiences," as one executive director said. "It involves finding ways within oneself to tolerate possible disagreements in political philosophy and operating styles."

All participants have conducted affirmative searches as they hire for new positions. Yet the real and imagined demands of working in a more diverse workplace raised anxieties and possibly contributed to high turnover. When it worked, those involved agreed that diversity added immeasurably to the standing of the foundation in its community, as well as to its performance in light of its mission.

Relations with the board also changed as the staff became more professional. With growth, foundation boards evolved from a working, volunteer-driven organization to a more policy-focused organization in which board members, typically in committee, developed policies to guide the day-to-day operations of the foundation, including personnel.

Those foundations with the greatest degree of staff accountability to the board followed a practice of annual staff performance reviews. Typically the executive committee or board chair reviewed the executive director, who in turn reviewed other staff. The most sophisticated foundations based their reviews on the person's contribution toward organizational goals specified in the foundation's growth plan and not solely on job descriptions.

Uses of technical assistance

Fortunately the growing pains experienced by these foundations were not suffered in isolation. Not only did executive directors come together annually to discuss progress and difficulties, the Leadership Program offered an assistance package to participants. This package, administered by the project director, was well-used and its availability created a climate of support needed to weather the turbulence of rapid growth.

The participants anticipated and appreciated their annual meeting. Typically held in January, each Round gathered separately for two days together. The executive director was usually invited, as well as the board chairperson or program officer. Each meeting meant sharing the year's highs and lows, the challenges and frustrations, the lessons learned and the unresolved dilemmas.

Also appreciated was the technical assistance allowance held by the project director for each participating community foundation, which designed its own mix of support (with approval). Examples of the variety of assistance the Program supported include:

- travel funds to allow community foundation staff to attend a project-related meeting, such as the annual meeting of the Children's Defense Fund;

- fees for a financial management consultant to review community foundation operations;

- travel and honorarium for a speaker for the community foundation's annual meeting, or a facilitator for its board or staff retreat;

- management training;

- purchases of computer hardware, software, and training.

Several specialized workshops were arranged and conducted for participants. Of special significance were workshops on "program-related investments" to which all three Rounds were invited, and a management clinic, convened especially for Round Two participants.

In a survey of participants on their uses of technical assistance (from any source, not just what was available through the Program), it was observed that the successive rounds of participants used more technical assistance. For Round One, the eight participants (combined) recorded 25 uses of technical assistance during their five years; the ten participants in Round Two recorded 35 uses during their first three years, and the nine participants in Round Three recorded 27 during its first year.

The two areas for which participants received the most technical assistance were administration/operations (30 uses) and programming/grantmaking (26), followed by financial resource development (19) and community role (12).

The most common mode of receiving technical assistance was in group workshops (35), particularly regarding programing/grantmaking; a consultant providing specific services to supplement staff (28), particularly in administration/operations; and individual consultation with staff or board (24), also in administration/operations.

In addition to technical assistance, each participant in Rounds One and Two received site visits in the first year by the project director, and in the first, second, and fifth year by the evaluator. These visits were occasions for actively reflecting on progress and its limitation, as well as for sharing some of the insights gained from recent visits to other participants. Round Three received site visits by the project director only. All these visits, as well as the entire package of assistance made available through the Program, were intended to support the development of participants' capacity.

As the project director stated, "In making this package of supportive assistance available, we created opportunities for each participant to become the best it could be." The value of this was affirmed by all. As one executive director said, "To my mind this aspect of the Program was most instrumental in supporting and sustaining our achievements."

Chapter Five

Taking on Capacity:
Leadership Skills

In this chapter we describe the demands of the
"catalyst" role of community leadership, the
factors that participants in the Leadership Program
considered in their choice of a community initiative,
and the basic features they designed into their
initiatives to "spark change" in their chosen area. We
then describe the enhanced capacities experienced
within the foundations themselves — increased skills
in their roles as catalyst, convener, and grantmaker.

Leadership skills:
A key ingredient of capacity

Skills, particularly leadership skills that help mobilize a community's commitment and constructively deploy its resources, are an essential component of community capacity.

In designing the Leadership Program for Community Foundations, the Ford Foundation recognized that local leadership is needed to address community problems. It recognized, too, that helping develop local leadership was a legitimate role for a national funder such as itself.

It was equally clear that a variety of community building groups play a role in becoming "part of the solution." These include groups and institutions that also have some degree of capacity themselves, and can contribute to community-wide problem solving. This includes government agencies, large corporations, small businesses, development organizations, neighborhood groups, volunteer organizations, charities, religious institutions, and even (or especially) families and individuals.

A number of things made community foundations special in the eyes of the Ford Foundation — aspects of their mission and position that make them well suited to play a highly constructive role in increasing the viability of communities:

- Governance by a group of community leaders charged with representing the interests of the community.

- Ability to play a neutral or non-partisan role in mobilizing commitments, to help "make something happen."

- Ability to bring people of different perspectives together to educate themselves on a community problem or opportunity, to formulate priorities, and to design and implement a cooperative or even collaborative response.

- Ability to develop philanthropic capital in the service of local problem solving and community building.

- Ability to put together a rational process to disburse grants and loans in support of a plan or program.

Development of these skills — named catalytic, convening, and grantmaking skills in the philanthropy field — became central to the purposes of the Leadership Program for Community Foundations. The Program gave its participants an opportunity to develop an initiative that would enable the community to address a significant problem.

Of the $100,000 given each year to those foundations chosen for the Program, up to $50,000 could be used to staff and support its initiative and its institutional growth, particularly its financial resource development. The remainder was to be allocated to grants or loans that would further the goals of the initiative. Each had the option of contributing to the initiative with its own money, raised for the purpose or granted from its discretionary funds.

Triggering change: The role of "catalyst"

To those community foundations chosen to participate, $500,000 seemed at first like a windfall. But it didn't take long for Program participants to recognize that award was not as much money as they (and all the resource hungry nonprofits in town) initially believed it to be.

These community foundations compared their $100,000 per year to the sums that still remained in local public budgets — the city's and county's — and regained perspective. Even though local public budgets had been decimated by Federal budget shifts, local line items for health, education, welfare, and community development still had millions, tens of millions, and even hundreds of millions of dollars per year. Even so, these public budgets were widely acknowledged as "inadequate to meet current needs."

It was fiscally impossible for community foundations to fill the gaps. Granting even $15,000 — a larger than average grant for these participants as they began the Program — to the general operations of an established nonprofit would do little to help it respond to the steadily increasing problems it faced.

The community foundations came to realize there was little they could do as funders "to meet current needs." Instead staff asked themselves, "How can we make these dollars go the farthest?" and "How can we best use these funds to bolster the community's ability to respond to this problem?"

The answers to these questions go beyond the solutions suggested by "more efficient service delivery," "good management," or "system coordination." Gaps in service delivery will always be with us, and the needs of people deemed needy will never be met.

Instead, the question, "How can we make these dollars go the farthest?" asks for ways to change the way things are done so that there are fewer needy and less demand for services. Changing the way things are done is the essence of the "catalytic" role that participating community foundations practiced in their leadership initiatives. A catalyst — a term from chemistry — is "an agent that increases the rate of change." Being a catalyst means "sparking change," which differs greatly from "meeting needs."

While meeting the needs of the needy is a vital task, many would argue that task is the province of charity and/or the public sector. Helping to reduce the number of needy people, or to change public and private responses so that fewer people become needy, is the province of institutions that wish to "make a difference" and "have an impact."

The distinction is revealed in an old aphorism, found framed on the wall of many foundations and other nonprofit organizations: "Give a man a fish, and he can eat for a day; teach him to fish and he can eat for a lifetime."

In our analysis, giving a hungry person a fish is charitable, for it reduces a need, though of course only momentarily. Teaching that person to fish is catalytic, for it allows that person to play a role as producer of solutions rather than as dependent consumer; it allows that person greater self-sufficiency. While both charitable and catalytic roles are necessary in a complex society, they are unmistakably different.

Community initiatives: The vehicle for "sparking change"

"A community foundation can't buy systems change," said one executive director, "but it can trigger it — and that's the challenge of the catalytic role."

But *how* to trigger change is one of the most persistent challenges facing all social institutions that want to make a difference, to remediate the problems of today's society, and to improve the quality of life for everyone.

How participants chose their initiatives

How did these community foundations choose an arena in which to play a leadership role? Just one issue of any daily newspaper reveals a variety of pressing problems and imminent crises. Resources to address these problems have been limited, and competition for attention and resources has been fierce.

Are certain issues more amenable than others to productive involvement by a small community foundation with limited resources? Can a community foundation attract discretionary contributions regardless of the issue chosen? What sort of politics go into making such a decision?

For Program participants, three major considerations were paramount in guiding choices: (1) payoff to the community; (2) support for taking on the issue; and (3) a constructive and appropriate role.

Payoff to the community. The issue should have meaningful benefits to large segments of the community. Foundation staff asked themselves and others these questions:

Is the issue highly significant to the whole community? All applicants spoke of the chosen issue as a major community issue, if not *the* community issue. Keeping current with issues and appraising their importance is one of the primary functions of a community foundation. It requires being in touch with a variety of sources: local government, planning organizations, community-based organizations and issue advocacy organizations.

Some issues chosen affected virtually all community residents: a fragile and threatened ecosystem, or a city stressed by racial and cultural alienation. Other issues, such as unwanted teen pregnancy or drug abuse, while directly affecting fewer people, threatened the future of the community.

Can the community foundation offer something immediately, as well as down the road? Several applicants wanted to create impact early in their involvement. They made grants early in hopes of raising the

117

foundation's visibility as a community leader, and to mobilize enthusiasm in the community. Such steps often proved helpful to the financial resource development work happening simultaneously.

Can the foundation help change the actual conditions that create the problems? Other applicants saw their primary usefulness as long-term, emphasizing education and prevention efforts, and public policy improvements. These efforts focused less on supporting the existing service delivery systems and more on supporting efforts to stem the flow of problem situations. A few participants looked specifically for an issue that would allow them to play a role in policy development.

Will the benefits be clear and meaningful? Designing a community initiative that produces easily communicated results is a major challenge. An initiative seeking to expand child care slots or educational opportunities can produce results that are easily understood and communicated.

Support for taking on the issue. Foundation staff had to assess whether the foundation had support for getting involved. Not all issues might be appropriate for community foundation involvement. They asked themselves and others these questions as a litmus test.

Do leaders in the area support the foundation's involvement? In offering leadership (as distinct from "taking" leadership), the community foundation had to be careful not to subvert or misdirect the existing leadership, but to build on it instead — and even then only if requested.

In each of these communities, foundation staff and sometimes board members met with many concerned and involved individuals and institutions to learn what type of involvement would be welcome. These checks extended to the elected, civic, and sometimes the grassroots leadership.

Do the foundation's own board members support its involvement? The choice of a specific issue was often responsive to the community (and philanthropic) interests of specific board members.

At each site, board members contributed a substantial proportion of the required match. Board members are the eyes and ears of the foundation in the community, and they also play a major role in soliciting contributions. While consensus or unanimity in the choice of issue was not an official requirement, it proved wise to poll members on their sense of an issue's suitability for the foundation and its potential for attracting funds.

Will our involvement in the issue attract funds for the community foundation? One major purpose of the Leadership Program was to develop the capacity of the community foundation as a resource in problem resolution, but perhaps even more so, as a developer of financial resources. Simply put, applicants had to choose an issue — and a confidence-building strategy for responding to the issue — that would attract funds.

The purpose of the Leadership Program's match requirement was to develop a local base of financial support. A scan of the policies and plans of nearby private foundations, corporate giving programs, local governments, and known philanthropists gave participants a reading of what other funders were doing — and not doing.

Most community foundations had at least a partial list of prospective donors in mind when they chose their initiative. Several knew they would target wealthy individuals, small family foundations and trusts. Others planned to target larger corporations and corporate foundations. Relatively "safe" issues — children, education and health — were chosen by several participants with these prospective donors in mind.

In a few instances, the choice of initiative was based on its potential for generating a broad base of public support, both for the issue and the foundation. Children and the environment proved to be viable themes.

Four years into the Program, not a single participant suggested that it had made the wrong choice of issue, or wished it had picked another. On the contrary, they said it was good for them, their community and those donors they'd originally had in mind.

A constructive and appropriate strategy. Choosing a good issue and designing a constructive strategy are two different things. It was not always obvious what role the community foundation should play to give useful leadership to an issue. Three criteria were useful in considering alternatives:

Is the foundation's involvement in this issue "appropriate"? While no one wanted to defer to "issue fadism," participants recognized the timing for their involvement could be wrong. Some avoided an issue that was highly polarized. One, however, saw it as an ideal opportunity to showcase the community foundation as a neutral force for resolution. Some would avoid an issue that seemed intractable and lacking in local leadership, but others wanted to highlight the community foundation's ability to to take on a difficult issue, forge a local consensus and galvanize different segments of the community into action. Some wanted to be recognized for persistent and long-term efforts in support of an issue, others saw their involvement as essentially a five-year commitment, and a small few wanted to be known for creating solutions and spinning them off to independent organizations.

Does the issue invite partnerships and collaboration? Because their own money could go only so far, several participants sought in the early months of participation to leverage that money — plus their leadership potential — to secure institutional resources and partnerships. Most participants developed cooperative relationships with local government and a variety of other community institutions. In almost every case, developing such an initiative was an opportunity to expand their relationships with a broader variety of organizations and constituencies, becoming more broadly based themselves in the process.

Does the issue allow other nonprofits to participate with maximum flexibility and creativity? This criterion, infrequently advanced, explicitly recognizes the missions of other nonprofit institutions and their roles. The Leadership Program offered community foundations a unique opportunity to help develop the capacities of a variety of nonprofit groups in their region.

Critical features of a community initiative

The challenge to community foundations — and to any kind of community organization — is to devise an initiative or program that creates the maximum impact with the scarce resources available.

How did participants in the Leadership Program translate the opportunity to play a leadership role into a program of action? This section focuses on the major working parts of their initiatives — the parts that they generally had in common — and critiques their advantages and disadvantages as experienced by participants. In Chapter Six we describe individual initiatives and their results.

These parts included: (a) staffing; (b) fact finding or background research; (c) a community advisory mechanism; (d) focused grantmaking; (e) community education and awareness efforts; (f) emphasis on system change, problem prevention, and raised levels of practice.

Staffing

Typically, how to staff the initiative was one of the first questions participating community foundations resolved. The first question was whether or not to hire someone. Should that person be a specialist on the initiative or a generalist who could serve as an all-around program officer? About half the participants chose to hire someone.

The participants who chose not to hire opted for the skills of a consultant, an outside agency contracted to staff the project, or a grant made to an outside agency to conduct much of the work. Four participants incorporated the work into the duties of existing staff.

The main reasons for hiring were that the community foundation needed specific expertise and/or that the community foundation's existing staff was already fully occupied. Those pursuing this tack found it satisfying, though a few had to hire a second time to get "the right person."

Most of the eight participants who hired a consultant found it rewarding, although there was a range of experience. For most it worked well because the expertise and routines developed by the consultant were integrated into existing staff functions, thereby bolstering the foundation's resident skills and visibility.

For a few it worked well for the opposite reason: the community foundation did not want the consultant's or outside contractor's work to become a routine function of the foundation. These community foundations wanted to be known for spinning off programmatic efforts rather than integrating and operating them. On the negative side, one community foundation's consultant failed to complete the work, throwing a heavier burden on an overworked staff. Another community foundation reported, "Some consultants have their own agenda."

The major advantages of proceeding without additional staff or consultant power were cost savings and opportunities for greater visibility for existing staff. "Stretching staff to the limit" has been reported with both optimism and skepticism. A lack of technical expertise to move beyond present levels of performance was also acknowledged.

Fact finding or background research

A majority of participating community foundations drew on some form of independent background research. This provided a mandate for their initiative and gave direction on how to proceed. In all but one case this work was commissioned by the foundation; and in one the research had been done by an independent agency as a "call to action" on behalf of the community at large, and the community foundation responded.

Uniformly, the experience of commissioning background research on an issue was a very positive experience. The exception was a consultant who didn't complete the work. Reported virtues included at least one of the following: (a) it helped to establish the issue as verifiably important; (b) it provided illustrations of how other communities responded to this particular problem; (c) it provided authoritative information on which to base the next steps; (d) it provided baseline data against which to measure progress.

A substantial advantage of commissioned research is that the finished product — typically a written report — was used to educate the community *and* mobilize community commitment. Written products were widely distributed and discussed in the media. Findings often became the basis of a forum as the community searched for solutions. In some instances, the report was attached to proposals for financial support.

Those who didn't commission independent research relied on their own committee discussions and/or staff-led discussions. A variety of community leaders was convened to educate them about the chosen issue. Sometimes this was done as part of the foundation's preparations for choosing an issue. Such discussions gave the foundation more visibility and extended networks, as well as providing a wealth of perspective. The occasional disadvantages were "information overload" and the time consumed.

About one-third of the participants drew both from independent research and their own discussions. This appeared to be the ideal combination. As noted in one comment, "The study we commissioned provided the credibility we needed. I can't imagine having done without it. The focus groups developed the necessary constituency support."

Community advisory mechanism

A substantial majority of participating community foundations wanted to "ground" their initiative formally in a wider, more community-based authority than the foundation alone carried. Two-thirds of participants created a special project advisory committee and half of the remainder used a pre-existing board committee, such as the distribution committee, for similar purposes. Relying solely on informal, one-on-one advice was the choice of only a few participants.

The major advantage of a special advisory committee, and to a lesser extent, the pre-existing distribution committee, was its ability to act as a mechanism for community ownership — or at least input and involvement — in the project. It was a vehicle for getting input from knowledgeable stakeholders, for gaining diversity of perspective, and for educating new levels of leaders and activists. Members helped forge community consensus, first among each other, and then among their constituents.

These committees developed priorities for action and recommended them to the community foundation, to the community at large, to their own institution, and to other key institutions. They helped design the next steps for the foundation, formed priorities for grantmaking and for demonstration projects, and helped move the agenda along.

Members helped educate different segments of the community about the activities of the foundation. Their own consensus was useful in mobilizing support for the issue, for developing additional resources and for forming new institutional linkages.

A sampling of testimony from participants includes: "This approach added a great deal of expertise that was not present on the foundation's board." "This approach gave broader exposure to the initiative, and the committee members provided valuable insights." "Our broad-based, very active and high level committee is what made the initiative so strong." "It positioned the foundation in developing a process for community impact."

While the conclusion was largely positive, some participants reported negative experiences: "The committee has worked very well, though I would reconsider the categories of membership." "Convening this group of volunteer leaders was both frustrating and worthwhile; as a group it was not very effective but it did build a network for the foundation in a new program area."

All participants using advisory committees reported benefits, principally the additional expertise and diversity of opinion that was gained.

The average number of advisory committee members, which is quite large, varies by Round: 69 for Round One participants in the first year for which we have data, 35 for Round Two and 17 for Round Three. These counts include *all* advisory committees, including those that advise the resource development and investment practices of the foundation.

The number of women and minorities serving on advisory committees has generally grown from year to year, but this growth has not been as fast as the overall growth in membership. Advisory committees are in fact slightly less diverse than they were earlier in the Program. The percent of advisory committee members that were female grew in Round One from 20 percent to 51 percent, and stayed nearly the same in Round Two, from 50 percent to 52 percent. The percent that were minority declined in Round One from 33 percent to 23 percent and declined slightly in Round Two from 29 percent to 23 percent.

It is likely that an analysis separating program advisory committees from financial advisory committees would show different diversity rates, with program advisory committees showing more diversity and increased diversity over time.

What *is* clear is that advisory committees are much more diverse than are the boards of these foundations. Conventional wisdom has suggested that advisory committees serve as arenas to scout talent that might do well on the foundation's board. However, in this study, only two advisors who were subsequently asked to serve on the board are known to Rainbow Research. It remains to be seen whether "advisorship" is allowed to grow into "governorship." How change happens in this arena is linked to the question, Which comes first, behavior change or attitude change? Do community foundations act themselves into a new way of thinking, or do they think themselves into a new way of acting?

Focused grantmaking

Two-thirds of the participating community foundations created a program of focused grantmaking. This typically meant staff created guidelines with priorities and eligibility criteria, announced the creation of such a program, and invited applications. They reviewed competing proposals, choosing those that best withstood a review process conducted by staff and advisory and/or distribution committee.

These programs were designed to achieve the outcomes articulated previously by an advisory committee or other fact finding effort. Typically, such programs were well presented and packaged, greatly aiding their attractiveness to donors and other funders.

Half of the foundations with targeted programs supported their grantees not only with money but with either pre-grant or post-grant technical assistance. Pre-grant technical assistance stands to strengthen applications by clarifying the intentions of the initiative to potential applicants. Post-grant technical assistance strengthens their chances for success by shoring up potentially weak areas and bringing in valuable resources. Both forms of technical assistance were appreciated by community foundation grantees, primarily because it helped create or affirm a relationship with the funder that went beyond monetary support.

Providing technical assistance also helps refine the community foundation's programmatic skills, because it requires a commitment to follow grantees' progress and learn about what helps them succeed, rather than "walking away" once the grant is made.

Almost half of those with targeted programs, and a few without them, invested substantially in "demonstration projects" and accompanying evaluation efforts. These are typically substantial investments in a frontal assault on the problem in an attempt to discover new solutions (or to reaffirm the value of established principles), and to draw major attention to the chosen issue.

A small but notable set of participants created non-targeted programs to fill in the cracks which became obvious once the targeted programs got underway, or to fill in the obvious cracks in other funders' programs.

A focused grantmaking program with limited funds is, by definition, unable to accomplish everything it might seek to undertake. The foundation must turn down proposals that have potential merit but are outside the expressed priorities. Some foundations took these "marginal" proposals to their donor advisors, providing an excellent occasion for donor education and cultivation. (See Chapter Three for the interplay between programming and financial resource development).

Community awareness and education

Most participating community foundations created efforts to educate the public on different aspects of their initiative or its results. Their purposes varied. Some wanted to create public awareness of the problems and opportunities the community was facing in the chosen issue area, and the priorities the foundation had developed in response. Still others hoped to showcase the foundation as a local leadership institution deserving of the community's support.

Participants were encouraged by the project director to use the media, beginning with guidance from Ford's communication department on writing press releases. Selection by the Ford Foundation into this Program and the $500,000 that came with it was newsworthy in all communities. Most participants parlayed this opportunity into more frequent contacts with local media. Many participants asked new grantees to write press releases, as well, which multiplied exposure of the initiative throughout the community and aided new grantees.

The communications efforts of participating community foundations greatly increased during the Program's five years with many more newsletters and announcements going out than previously. These supplied information about the initiative and other programs to three principal audiences: the community at large, prospective and current donors, and the nonprofit community. All foundations reported significantly greater visibility in their regions as a result of this Program's twin goals of financial resource development and leadership skill development.

Some awareness and education efforts were directed to the professionals or practitioners in the issue area rather than the general public. "Brown bag lunches," "forums," or "round tables" convened so that professionals or practitioners of different schools of thought, different geographic jurisdictions, or different service or funding systems could meet in a congenial setting.

The foundation's wish to help the community seek a higher common denominator for discussion fueled efforts to act as "neutral convener." By all accounts, the foundations got this wish. All were lauded for the "added value" their kind of leadership brought to the community.

Convening people when the purpose is to educate and share lessons (as distinct from creating a product) has the potential of increasing familiarity among potential partners and even raising hope (perhaps a precursor to "commitment") that something constructive can be done. It also helped clarify the role the foundation wished to play. In addition, it helped the foundation extend its network of informed practitioners and professionals.

System change, problem prevention, and improved practice

Consistent with the intent to produce the most long-lasting impact with the fewest dollars, most initiatives contained some elements that sought to (a) support changes in the policies that govern the way services are delivered; (b) focus the community on the value of prevention efforts over and above treatment efforts; (c) raise the standard of professional practice in the chosen issue area.

It takes a long time for most system change efforts to produce improved outcomes for intended beneficiaries. Just changing the system and its underlying politics takes a long time, even with no improvement in outcomes. Significantly, no one reported feeling that efforts in this direction were inappropriate for a community foundation, or a waste of time.

Prevention efforts in particular received a significant boost from community foundations, who saw the potential early due to fact finding efforts. "An ounce of prevention is worth a pound of cure" and like adages rang true. Foundations saw that "treatment" (of drug abuse or other dysfunctional behavior, for example) was the province of expensive professionals, bureaucratic systems and complicated third-party payment systems, whereas "prevention" encourages roles for the full gamut of community groups.

Raising the level of proficiency of service delivery system workers is another way to affect outcomes for whole groups of people rather than one person at a time. Five foundations focused work in this way, typically in the fields of early childhood education, day-care, or public education. Such efforts in which the skill level of day-care workers or school teachers and administrators is increased, are seen as key to improved quality and improved outcomes.

Results: Enhanced catalyst, convener, and grantmaking skills

The Leadership Program induced rapid skill development among its participants through the opportunity to implement a community initiative. The "catalyst, convener, and grantmaking roles" in particular became more defined and prominent, and helped participating community foundations play a more constructive role in their communities. In this section we examine growth in these three skill areas, deferring until the next chapter (Chapter Six) to amplify the results of each foundation's initiative and the major results it achieved.

Results and rewards of playing a catalytic role

It's while examining the catalytic role that Rainbow Research came to understand better the nature of community capacity, and the role of community foundations in contributing to its development.

In listening to hundreds of people during the course of this five-year evaluation at the eighteen sites of Rounds One and Two, we heard appraisals of what these foundations were accomplishing through initiatives.

On site we asked them, "What suggests you're gaining on the problem? What tells you that progress is being made?" We didn't ask for data suggesting that so-called problem indicators (such as adolescent pregnancy rates or school dropout rates) had decreased. They had not and probably would not for a while. Our focus was on the "sparking change" concept suggested by "catalyst."

We reminded our respondents that answers to this question often come at the end of the day or the week, when they feel either optimistic or pessimistic about their work. A question like, "What suggests you're on the right track, that pursuing this particular path strengthens this community in ways that *will* ultimately change the problem indicators?" elicited answers without ambivalence. The following reflects a composite answer:

"More and more people have become aware of this problem, have learned something about it, have become committed to doing something about it. The right people — people who need to be involved if anything's to happen, people in a position to influence other key people, people who were off in different directions competing and maybe even feuding — are now agreeing to some priorities and agreeing to help develop resources. In short, more people are committed.

"The foundation has raised money in the form of discretionary endowment, whose earnings can be deployed in this area. It has received grants from other funders and donors to increase the pool of funds it can give out in grants. Some of its donor advisors are interested in this issue. It has hired good staff who know the field, care about what groups are doing and want them to succeed. Staff helps educate the board on the issue it has chosen. The community foundation can give out money more easily than anyone else in town. It is learning through its advisors where small investments are most likely to produce the best results. Other funders have become interested and active in this arena. Groups and organizations that have received money from the community foundation are getting visibility and legitimacy, and find it easier to get money elsewhere. In short, there are more resources being deployed more intelligently to address the issue.

"More groups are being funded to do more worthwhile things. Many are getting additional help, especially with accessing expertise, equipment, or supplies they need. Many of these groups are getting help with planning, developing their management and project skills, and learning how the best in their field do things. Others are getting support for banding and working together to multiply their influence or to actively include still more groups and institutions in their work. In short, those community groups that are best positioned to move the problem indicators are getting more committed, more resourced, and more skilled."

We summarized the following as outcomes or "bottom lines" of community initiatives that make a difference:

- increased commitment to act, by broadening the ownership of solutions within key segments of the community, by enlisting more support for solving community problems, and by identifying more opportunities for action;

- expanded resources, financial and otherwise, available for addressing community problems, and improved means of getting money to groups that can use it in ways that are likely to be productive;

- strengthened community abilities to respond to problems and opportunities, by enhancing the skills of nonprofit organizations and volunteer groups, by assuring good programming and good management strategies, by encouraging stronger partnerships and collaborations, and by positioning the community foundation as an ally in these efforts.

We have shortened these to "commitment, resources and skills," the essential ingredients of community capacity. Enhanced community capacity is the major result of pursuing the catalytic role. Again, specific examples are provided in Chapter Six.

The art and craft of "convening"

The "convener" role is one of the leadership styles adopted by community foundations in this Program. The idea is simple: spokespeople for groups that are affected by a particular problem or are involved in finding solutions are brought together. These people are authorized to inform and advise the foundation on strategies for creating change. A hallmark of community leadership is bringing together people who can gain from each other's perspective and advice. Convening that gains consensus and lifts priorities is a practice that distinguishes community foundations from most other funding organizations.

Two-thirds of the participants in all three Rounds created a project advisory committee, an act of convening in itself. Participating community foundations learned a great deal from their committees. Their skills in convening developed in the following ways.

Foundations learned to get advice from diverse perspectives. Participating community foundations learned to include: (a) representatives of the diverse viewpoints, constituencies, and organizations that could play constructive roles; (b) people who could access needed resources — financial and otherwise; and (c) people in a position to strengthen the capacities or enhance the influence of organizations, associations, and groups that could play a constructive role.

All participants noted that inviting and considering new and diverse points of view added strength and quality to the product. It also expanded knowledge of the resources available in the community and created new information streams.

Foundations learned to be clear about the advisory committee's authority and what was expected from it. Some learned the hard way what happens when clarity is in short supply. Advisory committees may assume they are "governing bodies" or "decision-making bodies" unless informed that they can make recommendations — but not decisions — for the foundation.

What *can* be expected is a set of recommendations for strategies the foundation can pursue to help the community make progress. Recommendations typically focused on the types of goals or efforts to fund, people to involve, resources to gather and community education to undertake.

If the committee lacked a product orientation *and* the guidance of a foundation staff person or committee chairperson, it tended to degenerate into a discussion group without direction. Often the effective committee chairperson was an interested community foundation board member who stepped forward to act as liaison to the initiative's advisory committee.

Foundations learned the value of "staying neutral." Respondents said, "The community foundation's value to the community, especially in the formulation of the initiative, lay in the fact that it 'had no ax to grind,' and 'no vested interest in a particular organization or solution'." Some participants have noted that this idea of "neutrality" is perhaps overstated. They say that neutrality is lost when a set of funding priorities is developed, when the foundation's "position" is identifiable through those priorities. Other directors note that what is neutral is the process — the foundation led a fair process that resulted in a set of priorities fashioned with the input of multiple stakeholders.

Foundations learned how to move the committee beyond talk to action. This was aided by: a) clarifying *why* the group was convened and, in particular, what kind of product was expected of it; b) focusing on and isolating key ingredients of a successful initiative, or an itemization of "what progress ought to look like in this community"; c) helping the group develop priorities for community education, resource development, capacity building and grantmaking; d) facilitating the planning, enhancing the group's own capacities as a working partnership, tracking progress, and keeping people at the table; e) financing progress on the group's principal recommendations.

Convening was not limited to convening advisory committees. Convening also refers to the practice of facilitating connections or relationships among people who should connect to pave the way for progress. Because of the community foundation's reputation as a neutral or fair institution, it could bring people together in ways that more partisan institutions could not.

This practice reinforced the community's perception of its foundation as a leader of fair-minded, goal-directed, community-focused discussions. Success begot opportunity. The foundation was invited to more discussions, and to host more discussions.

Some drawbacks to convening as a leadership style were noted. Formal advisory committees can be costly to operate, especially if they meet frequently, receive assignments, and require staff support between meetings. They require logistical support, including regular and timely communications, calendar coordination, meeting space, refreshments, and a plan to reimburse travel and child care costs.

Other difficulties surfaced, though briefly. First, unless there's innovative outreach to recruit new blood, advisory committees display "the same old people" and the "same old politics." Second, election year politics and city or county squabbling over turf had negative effects on some committees. Third, when grant money was at stake, the community foundation had to guard against possible conflicts of interest. A policy addressing such a conflict should be in place *before* it needs to be invoked. Fourth, the advisory process should allot members and staff time to educate themselves prior to making decisions on an issue, so that they act with commonly held information.

Proactive, reactive, and interactive grantmaking

Grantmaking in support of a community initiative — when certain goals are held up as priorities — is done differently than grantmaking under other circumstances. It is essentially the difference between "proactive" or "strategic" grantmaking, and "reactive" or "responsive" grantmaking.

Proactive or strategic grantmaking proceeds from an intention "to make something happen" with scarce resources. A proactive grantmaker typically works from a set of priorities — priority strategies it wants to activate, priority target groups or areas it wants to include or impact, priority outcomes it wants to achieve. It announces these, inviting groups to submit proposals describing how they would, given the opportunity, do the work that the funder wants to encourage.

Reactive or responsive grantmaking, on the other hand, supports the general purpose of "service to the community." It assumes that good ideas, good organizations and good leadership already doing good work abound, and that what they need most is more financial support. Typically, a responsive grantmaker invites proposals of a general nature, or in areas in which it has a professed interest. It may have guidelines to help it weed out ineligible organizations and others to separate meritorious proposals from the rest.

Responsive or reactive grantmaking has an important, though more passive, role in community capacity building. It can be effective at accomplishing the purposes of applicant organizations, which presumably have legitimate purposes. A very good case can be made for funding worthwhile organizations simply because they *are* worthwhile.

A community foundation may practice both proactive and reactive styles of grantmaking in different program areas. Assertive leadership pushing to make a difference may be most appropriate in some areas. In others, sufficient and effective leadership may be in place, requiring primarily financial support. The appropriate terms may well be proactive and reactive grantmaking *programs* rather than proactive and reactive *funders* .

But the intent in this Program was "to help a community address a problem or issue." That goal, as defined by the Program's designer, is aided when a foundation decides — and is equipped — to develop its skills as a catalyst. Ideally, the agenda that emerges has been defined through the community advisory process described above, making it "the community's work." That was the expectation of the participating community foundations. To describe this style of grantmaking we could introduce a third term — "interactive grantmaking" — which recognizes that the community foundation's goals are not uniquely its own but have been fashioned in interaction with stakeholders. It suggests the goals are shared with those voices at the table that contributed to the formulation of those goals. Almost all of the participants in this Program practiced this interactive style of grantmaking.

More sophisticated grantmaking

Most participants created several enhancements to their grantmaking practices. Making these changes helped them become more effective in achieving the initiative's goals, more efficient in the use of staff and board time, and more accountable to community constituents.

Improvements in these four areas were noted: (a) guidelines for projects and programs; (b) publicity and outreach mechanisms; (c) grant review process; and (d) board/committee involvement.

One might think that with these types of changes that these community foundations became more bureaucratic, but this was not the case. In interviews on site we heard considerable testimony from nonprofit and public partners that the community foundation gives quicker turnaround and more helpful consideration to requests than any other local funders.

Enhanced guidelines for projects and programs. Most participants made one or both of these types of changes to enhance the way their projects and programs are communicated to those seeking support: (a) The community foundation more clearly specified the types of efforts and outcomes it wanted to support. (b) The community foundation reduced the number of different programs in-house, often by establishing an overarching theme to embrace them all, resulting in a more coherent and recognizable focus.

Benefits noted: (a) Guidelines allow the distribution committee to target resources against a specific vision, and the committee has a more consistent basis on which to judge an application's strengths and weaknesses. (b) Grant applicants also have a better basis for preparing applications; they can specifically address topics of concern to the foundation. (c) The board becomes more enthusiastic and supportive as members see their grantmaking having an impact on particular broad-based issues. (d) Focus allows participants to attract outside resources more easily. (e) The lessons learned in one area of community foundation interest are seen more easily to apply to others. (f) Stating expectations broadly allows the foundation to provide more options for support, such as technical assistance and program related investments. (g) More focused applications allow staff and board to more quickly assess what the applicant hopes to accomplish and how.

Improved publicity/outreach mechanisms. Changes made to the way the foundation makes known its opportunities for support, and to whom: (a) Participants held publicized workshops to inform possible applicants and partners of new initiatives and changes in guidelines. (b) Guidelines were printed on brochures that can be mailed. (c) The foundation's mailing list becomes useful for informing the community of its priorities and interests.

Benefits noted: (a) A broader array of organizations know what the foundation does and wants. (b) The quality of proposals is greatly improved.

Enhanced grant review process. Changes made to improve the efficiency of the grant review process: (a) The foundation hired a staff person to review discretionary grant applications; later, several of these foundations were able to hire a grants assistant (sometimes their second) to manage the paperwork. (b) Staff did more and better work-up for each grantmaking cycle, giving better materials to the distribution committee. (c) Some foundations added grant cycles, some reduced, some consolidated; no clear verdict on the "right" number of grant cycles emerged, though most have settled on two-three per year. (d) Some went to a two-stage review process, requiring first a letter of intent from potential applicants, and then if warranted, a fully developed proposal.

Benefits noted: (a) Staff time and expertise is better used, from executive director down. (b) The board gets better analysis and investigation of grant options, with staff more focused on the objectives of the initiative. (c) Better assistance is given to grantees. (d) More staff means foundation can handle more requests, and still give quick turnaround. (e) Grant review process is now more equally shared by staff and distribution committee (or advisory committee), which mixes valuable expert advice and community input. (f) Letters of intent encourage staff/applicant consultations, assistance, greater congruence of interest and capability. (g) Consultations strengthen the quality of grants as well as relationships in community.

Enhanced board/committee involvement. Changes made to the way board members or advisors can involve themselves in the foundation's programs and projects: (a) The board created an advisory committee for the initiative to help staff formulate guidelines and review applications; sometimes there were one-two board members on this committee as liaison, and sometimes the committee was chaired by a board member. (b) The advisory committee was constituted with greater diversity of representation than the board typically was. (c) Volunteer committee members accompanied staff on site visit. (d) More board members served for a period on the distribution committee, (e) Staff sent an improved docket of materials to the committee (or board) ahead of their meetings, including staff assessments of the application's quality, and recommendations if requested.

Benefits noted: (a) Broader community involvement brings broader perspective to the board. (b) Board liaison to the advisory committee allows the board to feel more confident in the judgments of the committee. (c) Diversity on the advisory committee gives access to minority or non-traditional segments of the community to the community foundation. (d) Diversity on the advisory committees gives staff a chance to scout new talent for additional foundation roles. (e) Staff benefit from volunteers' perspective, and staff presence provides consistency across the board. (f) Committee discussion is more focused, concerned with appropriate details. (g) Board members on distribution or advisory committees can play a more informed role, guided by the foundation's own criteria. (h) The board is more interested in the mission of the community foundation and members become better spokespeople for the foundation and its role in the community.

Dilemmas in discretionary grantmaking

Discretionary grantmaking, precisely because it demands the exercise of discretion, can be both alluring and perplexing. Having choices creates dilemmas, where opportunity and responsibility are difficult to balance.

The major issues relate to the terms and conditions of grants, particularly continuation grants; the nature of the relationship between foundation and grantee, particularly when the goals of each are shared; and scaling the foundation's resources to the scale of potential grantees' capabilities.

These issues are illustrated below, in a sample of counterpoints that distribution committees found themselves grappling with after a few short but filled years of experience with a major community initiative:

"Now that we have more discretionary money to give out, it might be better to give fewer but larger grants, because with larger grants we might see more impact."	*Versus*	"We're getting good at making 'small' grants, and have learned about the sort of organizations and situations in which they work well."
"We really want these grantee organizations to succeed, and we have a lot of ways to support them in achieving their goals."	*Versus*	"We don't want to crowd or unduly influence our grantees or otherwise suggest we don't respect their ability to do a good job."
"We'll give second-year grants only to those groups that prove they've done a good job."	*Versus*	"We've chosen groups we believe can play a constructive role, and will support their growth until they've reached the next level of development."

"When this project's five-year timeline runs out, we can move on to another initiative."	*Versus*	"When this project's five-year timeline runs out, let's make sure the gains made are not lost."

One heard in these committee discussions both the excitement that such meaningful issues induces, and the frustration of having too little information to guide a resolution.

A small handful of participants were beginning to develop the information that could guide resolution to these dilemmas, largely from their own grantees. Given the intensity with which these initiatives were undertaken, these participants felt it important to learn whether their grantees were succeeding in their efforts, what sort of difficulties they were experiencing (so that support can be sent in), and what their successes were (so that they can tell others). Sometimes this information was developed through formal, written reports by an independent evaluator, but more illuminating and beneficial to all was its development by convening grantees in reflective discussion. Nevertheless, developing this information was rare, and rarer still was forwarding it to advisory and distribution committees for their edification and planning.

It is possible that such steps might be taken if the Program were six years rather than five in duration, that it takes extra time to "close the loop" such that advisors become steeped in knowledge of results so they can plan the steps that could help grantees — and the segments of the community they work with — get to the next level of capacity. This is the edge at which most community foundations in the Leadership Program found themselves in their fifth and last year of participation.

Chapter Six

Building Capacity:
The Results of
Community Initiatives

In this chapter, we summarize the results of the
community initiatives undertaken by participants in the
Leadership Program for Community Foundations.
Specifically, we highlight three major outcomes achieved
through their efforts: increased commitment, expanded
resources, and strengthened skills. We then provide profiles
of the initiatives undertaken by Program participants,
highlighting their accomplishments in these three areas.

The results of community initiatives

Initiatives are only the beginning. In the last chapter, structural characteristics of a community initiative, as well as the major roles that community foundations play in carrying them out, were examined.

In this chapter, three major results that could be directly attributed to these initiatives are described. In on-site interviews, Rainbow Research staff asked, "How can you tell you're gaining on the problem? What tells you that progress is being made?" We knew not to ask for evidence that teen pregnancy rates had dropped, or that employment rates had risen. Those outcomes, if ever achieved, could be better attributed to actions taken by other players, either downstream of the community foundation (prospective parents, employers), or upstream (federal policy, global economics), or in a different stream altogether (fate, providence).

But what indicators told of progress or gains? We asked our respondents (board, staff, advisors/volunteers, grant recipients, partners to local initiatives, and knowledgeable bystanders without direct involvement in the community foundation) that question directly and developed three major outcomes. These reflect the gains made through successful efforts of a community foundation in leading an initiative. Indeed, we propose they are emblematic of a successful community initiative, and we propose they serve as the keystone of the concept of community capacity, as introduced in Chapter One.

These three major outcomes are:

The community's commitment to act was increased. Progress in building healthy communities requires people and institutions work together in ways that call on their strengths and invite them to contribute. Since different people and institutions bring different qualities to this task, one role of the community foundation is to help articulate and mobilize these contributions. One encouraging sign of progress is an informed consensus among different segments of the community on how to focus resources and skills to create solutions and strengthen community talent.

The community's pool of resources was expanded. Making progress typically requires resources, with financial resources to invest in building healthy communities at the top of the list. Other resources include guidelines on how best to spend money, include information on opportunities that promise to be productive, and guidelines for investing or allocating resources fairly.

The capacity building skills of community's groups' were strengthened. People and institutions other than the community foundation ultimately have to become more productive with their chosen work. Such community groups benefit from increased commitment, resources, and skills, too, and their work requires they increase the capacity of others near them and so on and on, from one group to another. Virtually all groups and organizations need additional skills to help them reach the next level of capability. Respondents reported progress when they saw nonprofit and civic partners with constructive roles to play adding to their skills.

We will explore each of these themes in greater detail, positing some subthemes that emerged from the initiatives undertaken in this Program, naming particular community foundations that provided illustrations of that outcome. Later in the chapter we profile the initiative undertaken by each community foundation participating in Rounds One and Two of the Leadership Program for Community Foundations.

Increased commitment

Advisory committee members educated themselves and the community foundation on an important community issue. Advisory committees were convened and given encouragement to educate themselves on the ins and outs of a particular community issue. The opinions and expertise of community leaders, service delivery system representatives, local government, business groups, and professionals were freely exchanged, and influenced the community foundations grantmaking guidelines (Dayton, Memphis, Southeastern Michigan, Rochester, Madison, Central New York). The opinions of neighborhood leaders were sought before developing grantmaking guidelines affecting neighborhoods (Richmond), and the leaders in the *colonias* were consulted before developing guidelines affecting them (El Paso). "Regional Roundtables" were held to explore the concept of acting regionally, in transportation, for example (Triangle).

The broader public, or segments of it, were informed of productive courses of action. Public education and awareness efforts were a part of several initiatives (Arizona, Dayton, El Paso, Memphis, Baltimore, Lorain, Tucson). For example, through a new curriculum, school children learn about their region's environment and how to steward it (El Paso). Legislators were approached and informed of priorities for making the state more child-friendly (Arizona, Greenville, Baltimore, Central New York). Business leaders were shown how the business climate was affected by their community's family health (Arizona, Greenville, Baltimore, Central New York).

People were given the opportunity to be heard in a way that expanded their influence. Reactions to specially commissioned studies or proposals were solicited before shaping guidelines for action (Rochester, Lorain). A study done by a grassroots organization was promoted and made central to funding efforts (Greenville).

Commitments to act were sought and secured from those in a position to influence. Candidates for governor debated the issues of children, and promises were secured through advocacy

147

efforts (Arizona, Tucson). School and business officials became committed to supporting efforts to upgrade the county's public schools (Lorain). The business community developed "family-friendly" policies and models with the help of child advocates and promoted them among its ranks (Baltimore).

Broad-based coalitions of community leaders in support of productive activity were built. Building coalitions of substantial numbers of organizations or individuals to influence public policy were a part of a few initiatives (Arizona, Tucson, Baltimore).

Expanded resources

"Good efforts" or "exceptional people" were more visible to other potential supporters. Programs deemed by the community foundation to be "excellent" received publicized awards and/ or longer term funding to position them to attract more financial resources, create political standing, and strengthen organizational development (East Tennessee, Memphis, El Paso). Most participants provided publicity through newsletters, annual meetings, or press releases to organizations playing particularly beneficial roles.

Funds or other resources were attracted to the community foundation's efforts. Most participants raised additional money from other sources to supplement the grantmaking dollars provided by the Program. Many will likely continue their initiative well past the five-year life of the Program through an intentionally expanded base of financial support (Arizona, Dade, Dayton, El Paso, Southeastern Michigan, Baltimore, Lorain, Madison, New Orleans, Tucson).

Other funders increased their contributions. Funding by the community foundation served as an important imprimatur that served the grantee who looked for funding elsewhere; this was especially true early in the group's organizational life (Memphis, New Orleans, Richmond, East Tennessee). Funding by the community foundation also helped make "risky" topics or groups more acceptable to other funders. Private and corporate foundations as well as city government appreciated that the community foundation was working and listening "out there, close to the ground." Several projects or partnerships vitally helped by the community foundation were later supported by other funders.

Allocation processes were improved so that less money can be wasted. The "priorities" for funding recommended by advisors intend, by definition, to direct scarce monies to do the most good. With adopted priorities, grant review committees could benchmark their reviews against these priorities, directing more money to priority efforts. Applicants given pre-grant assistance, and visited on-site by staff and committee members experienced reduced subjectivity and increased support for meritorious efforts.

Approaches were identified that can make resources go farther or have more impact. "Raising the level of practice," as distinct from "providing for services directly," required less money and had more enduring effects (Rochester, Central New York, Greenville). Helping to "remove barriers to economic self-sufficiency" rather than providing training or counseling directly followed the same rationale (Dayton). "Initiating partnerships among existing resources" defused the impulse to start a new program to help at-risk kids (Madison). "The keys to effective prevention" were identified and then incorporated into requests for proposals, to ensure that scarce money be used to purchase what's known to work (Arizona, Southeastern Michigan, Memphis, Tucson). A map showing the location of family health-engendering resources revealed parts of town that were short on resources (Tucson). Strengthening weak organizations that attempt to help recipients get off welfare would take less money than working directly with such people (Northwest). Building information sharing networks among grantees allows them to enter cooperative arrangements and focus institutional resources better (East Tennessee).

New philanthropic endowments were created. Each participating community foundation raised $1 million minimum in new permanent funds whose earnings could be deployed at the discretion of its board to build community capacity.

The uses of funds were advised by a broader base of voices. The issues chosen for community initiatives affected a broad range of people, particularly those with fewer options and financial resources. Since the advisory committees or distribution committees of these community foundations had a greater diversity of people (primarily with respect to gender, race, income, and vocation) than their governing boards, foundation resources reached a greater variety of useful groups than might have been achieved otherwise.

Strengthened skills

Links among like-minded groups or organizations were strengthened. Some participants facilitated the exchange of information across traditional boundaries by convening groups to discuss common issues and new strategies, or by supporting groups with successful ventures to spread their knowledge to those who could use it (Dade, Southeastern Michigan, East Tennessee, Triangle). Some supported new forms of partnering, cooperating, and collaborating among nonprofit partners (Dade, Dayton, Lorain, Madison, Triangle, Tucson). Some experimented with new institutional arrangements with other funders (Arizona, Dayton, Memphis, Rochester, Madison, Richmond, East Tennessee, Tucson).

New and emerging leadership was encouraged. A new, formal program encouraged leadership from a regional perspective (Triangle). Neighborhood level leadership was cultivated to spark the development of affordable housing (Richmond). A few participants encouraged leadership through newly formed coalitions (Baltimore, Arizona), professional groups (Baltimore, Central New York, Lorain), or partnerships among grantees (Dade).

The management and technical skills of organizational part-ners were strengthened. Some participants made a point of bringing in or supporting "technical assistance" for their nonprofit partners, to aid in their project or organizational development (Greenville, New Orleans, Central New York, Richmond, Spokane, East Tennessee, Tucson). One participant created a "center for ex-cellence" to help upgrade the skills of all those involved with pub-lic education in the county (Lorain).

The quality of service or level of practice in a community group or delivery system was improved. Raising standards of practice in a given field and helping practitioners achieve desirable skill levels helped some communities make progress (Greenville, Rochester, Central New York). Helping groups adopt approaches known to work helped others (Southeastern Michigan, Arizona, East Tennessee, Lorain).

Eighteen initiatives and their results

In this section we will describe each of the initiatives undertaken by the eighteen participating foundations in Rounds One and Two.

Given limited space, we've kept these short, and have linked the three ingredients of community capacity to the prominent outcomes of each foundation's initiative. Each description is pro-ceeded by language from annual reports or brochures describing each community foundation's mission and community role.

Arizona Community Foundation
Phoenix

Stephen D. Mittenthal, President

Commitment

Resources

Skills

The mission of the Arizona Community Foundation has five key ingredients: "To develop a permanent endowment from multiple sources of philanthropic capital; to use the income from that endowment to respond to emerging and changing community needs; to provide a vehicle for donors to exercise their varied charitable interests; to provide prudent stewardship of assets gifted by donors; to serve as a catalyst, neutral convener/broker and change agent for community betterment."

First envisioned as a Children's Mental Health initiative, the Foundation expanded and restated its scope in the second year to "Children at Risk." Early on, Arizona Community Foundation created a statewide Arizona Children's Campaign "to bring about a statewide public policy change that will provide the greatest benefit for the most children." Co-sponsored by Arizona Community Foundation, the Children's Action Alliance (an advocacy and policy research group), and the Children's Defense Fund, the campaign developed and publicized a "Platform for Arizona's Children" and "Legislative Priorities" for the state. The campaign made children's issue the subject of public debate in the highest echelons of the private and public sector, inducing commitments on behalf of children from both major candidates for governor.

Arizona Community Foundation co-sponsored creation of The Arizona Children's Trust Fund, "the first privately capitalized state-wide endowment for children." It is structured as a field-of-interest endowment fund held in both the Arizona Community Foundation and Tucson Community Foundation, but is marketed statewide very publicly, with special brochures, sponsors, mailings, and campaign. Within five years the Children's Trust Fund had raised $3.2 million from around the state.

Arizona Community Foundation commissioned a study in Year One that synthesized and articulated the key ingredients of successful prevention efforts. This list guided the Foundation's shopping for five projects ($260,000) that demonstrated these principles in prevention and early intervention efforts for children "at risk" of mental illness.

By Year Four, advocacy, prevention, and system change had become the triple anchor for Foundation programming in the children's field. A second grant in 1991 from the Ford Foundation to Arizona Community Foundation and the Tucson Community Foundation helped to create the "Partnership for Children," a public/private coalition including the Tucson Community Foundation and the Office of the governor. Its purpose: to help reshape children's services in Arizona through a policy and structural reform process and through expanding the Arizona Children's Campaign of public education and legislative advocacy into Southern Arizona.

Commitment

Resources

Skills

Dade Community Foundation
Miami

Ruth Shack, President

Dade Community Foundation maintains endowments to be used to benefit the people of Greater Miami. Its goals are "to expand its permanent, discretionary community endowment; to provide an independent flexible vehicle for donors' varied interests; to support local philanthropy through informed stewardship, enhancing grant support with other resources and services; to address pervasive problems and changing needs by aggregating multiple sources of philanthropic trusts."

Dade's leadership theme of "cultural alienation" began with discussions convened just as Ruth Shack began her role as executive director, asking "What could the Dade Foundation do to make a difference in the complicated, multi-ethnic, multi-cultural system that is Dade County?" Rather than pick a single problem, the Foundation decided to use all its resources to build a more cohesive, less alienated Miami.

Three different grantmaking programs were developed as part of its five year effort. First came Miamians Working Together, which made grants to 11 community-based organizations to launch teen businesses which involved youth but with clients or customers ethnically different from themselves. Then came Miami Art Bridge, to fund cultural arts groups to conduct intercultural activities, performances or events. Then came a three-year program to support grassroots neighborhood associations in tackling neighborhood problems first in South Dade, and then later in North and Central Dade through the community foundation's participation in the C.S. Mott's Foundation's "Community Foundations and Neighborhoods Small Grants Program."

Growing alongside these grantmaking programs were strategies to improve grantees' effectiveness. Requests for Proposals along with workshops informed the community of specific programmatic objectives and helped to create sharper proposals. Technical assistance and management support to grantees offered by culturally appropriate organizations became a staple of Foundation offerings intent on bolstering capacity of organizations working to foster community cohesion.

"Building a cohesive community" became the priority of all the Foundation's discretionary grantmaking beginning in Year Three, and the community foundation committed to making its board and staff mirror the complexion of the area. One hallmark of its style is to import philanthropic capital from afar, and route it directly down to grassroots levels. Ford Foundation provided $500,000 to launch the Partnership for Community and Economic Development to create low cost housing, new businesses and new opportunities, and another $250,000 to support key local organizations in their strategic planning. Rockefeller Foundation provided $450,000 for high school humanities activities in the public schools designed to reduce prejudice and break down racial barriers. At home, Dade Community Foundation has influenced other local funders, and doubled its assets between the time it embraced this theme and the end of its participation in this Program, suggesting its position and work has been well regarded.

Commitment

Resources

Skills

The Dayton Foundation
Ohio

Frederick Bartenstein, III, Director (until September 1991)
Darrell Murphy (1992 —)

Commitment

The mission of The Dayton Foundation is "to meet changing needs and improve the quality of life in the Dayton/Miami Valley region through the development of community philanthropy." In a unique statement of values, "The Dayton Foundation will provide excellent, balanced and responsive service to its primary constituents — donors, nonprofit organizations and the community at large. The Foundation accepts a special responsibility to initiate and encourage actions likely to produce long-term benefits for the region. The Foundation is a vehicle for the generosity of its many donors, not the object of their generosity."

Resources

Dayton's Self-Sufficiency Program was a five-year effort to develop strategies and programs to address the issue of economic independence and to remove barriers for young adults in Montgomery County.

In the first year The Dayton Foundation created a Project Governing Board of influential leaders, which met continuously for five years (and continues to meet). In its first two years it heard presentations from practitioners and policy makers bearing on issues of structural unemployment, and formulated a shared perspective. They developed a set of "barriers to self-sufficiency" against which they could design projects and target resources.

Skills

A brief video focusing attention upon the at-risk population and explaining what's meant by "barriers to self-sufficiency" was produced for use with local service clubs, chambers of commerce, and other groups in a position to chip away at barriers for the benefit of the community. A group of unemployed or underemployed persons were tracked in a four-year study, and provided information about particularly troublesome barriers, coping strategies, and opportunities for barrier removal efforts.

If barriers are the problem, barrier removal is the solution, the board reasoned. Pilot projects and policy initiatives were developed to find weaknesses in the structure of structural unemployment, so that they could be breached by innovative practices. One study found the value of a battery of intensive support services provided to General Assistance recipients in helping them become competitively employed and retain jobs. Another project placed qualified AFDC clients in jobs at sites where the personnel offices have been persuaded to suspend the usual screening devices, which had proved to be barriers to employment even among qualified applicants. Others were developed for literacy, utility bills arrearage, substance abuse coordination, and improved assessment of an individual's needs and resources. All these projects attracted additional funding and support from appropriate county or state agencies as well as the local business community. The "barrier removal" metaphor has proven useful as it helped community leaders direct attention to the effects of various public and private practices in the labor market rather than on "the problem with people these days." It has also proven difficult to translate from metaphor to practice because decades of social welfare policy and human service professionalism has focused on fixing people rather than fixing systems.

Towards the end of Year Five, The Dayton Foundation along with the United Way and Montgomery County's Human Services Levy joined forces to create a Self-Sufficiency Project Fund, advised by the the Self-Sufficiency Program Board — by then a highly informed and effective collaboration of community leaders — to continue to search for opportunities to lower barriers to sustained employment.

Commitment

Resources

Skills

El Paso Community Foundation
Texas

Janice W. Windle, President

The philosophy of El Paso Community Foundation is unique: "We strive to protect and enhance the unique resources of El Paso — its diversity of race and culture, its richness of artistic creation and appreciation, and the beauty and quality of its desert, land, air, and water, so that these resources may be enjoyed now and in the future. We are committed to the equality of opportunity for all and the elimination of any injustice, prejudice or indifference that denies or delays its attainment. We seek to enhance human dignity by providing support for community members to exercise personal responsibility and to participate actively in determining the course of their own lives and the life of the community. We seek to establish mutual trust, respect and communication among the foundation, its grantees and the community within which they operate. We will respond to the creative impulses of organizations and individuals as they seek to address the opportunities and dilemmas of changing community needs and interests. We are committed to using the resources entrusted to us for the funding of diverse projects, recognizing that issues are often complex, interdependent and changing. We will seek out new and creative approaches to solving problems as well as methods that are tried and effective. We recognize that the process of change and enhancement often involves a partnership of individuals, groups and institutions. We will be an active partner in that process as member of the philanthropic community. The El Paso Community Foundation is a steward through which private assets entrusted to us by generations of donors are invested to meet the challenges of contemporary life. We are committed to the belief that a community foundation exists to solve community problems and to promote the right of every American to participate in philanthropy."

The Foundation's "Living on the Desert" initiative is less an initiative on a problem or issue, and more a theme or banner that allows the foundation to help those in its region focus on "place," a

Commitment

Resources

Skills

158

subtext to "community" that too seldom gets explored, particularly by funders. "Living on the desert" is a theme that bonds El Pasoans.

The centerpiece of "Living on the Desert" is the development of an earth-science curriculum for grades three through eight. The film-based curriculum is designed to instill leadership skills and responsibility in the community's future leaders. The films were made by award winning writers and film makers. Six local science teachers wrote an earth-sciences curriculum following Texas educational requirements. Now, for two weeks each year, El Paso children can focus directly on the environment of their specific region — a perspective that "national" textbook publishers consistently omit. The curriculum consists of a videotape portion, teachers' guides, and extra enrichment materials.

The curriculum has been adopted in fourteen school districts in Far West Texas, both public and private. Thanks to classroom discussion and home assignments, their teachers and families are also better equipped to be stewards of their region's fragile environment. A mini-grants program for teachers encourages them to submit innovations to the curriculum already in place; a committee selects up to six for cash awards, and the winning additions to the teachers' guides are then promoted for use. As an investment that continuously repays, the cost per child of developing the curriculum is amortized indefinitely.

Supplementary grant, loan, and awareness programs support efforts to improve water quality and health conditions in the region.

El Paso Community Foundation's interest in the environment and its location on the border with Mexico allows it to operate bi-nationally. The Foundation collaborates with other foundations, local and federal governments, universities, and corporations on both sides of the border to strengthen local responses to local issues.

Commitment

Resources

Skills

Community Foundation of Greater Greenville
South Carolina

James B. Richmond, President (until July 1988)
Jack Cromartie, President (early 1989 —)

The mission of the Community Foundation is "to enhance the quality of life of the community in these ways: as a resource developer, building a permanent discretionary endowment and providing services to donors, nonprofit organizations and the community at large; as a steward, receiving, managing and distributing community resources; as a grantmaker, providing direct financial resources to targeted programs that address immediate or emerging community issues; and as a community resource, developing coalitions and mobilizing community leaders and constituencies."

The "Greenville's Child" initiative was launched after a two-year study of local child care needs carried out earlier by local civic and church groups. The four primary objectives were to develop and promote a centralized child care information and referral network for parents; to initiate joint programs between agencies and area educational institutions for pre-service and in-service training of child care center personnel; to expand available child care for low income families; and to implement a public awareness and public policy campaign targeted at long term issues of child care quality and child care center licensing and safety.

The centerpiece of this effort was the creation of a new nonprofit organization, also called Greenville's Child, which essentially took on the four objectives of the initiative. In addition, the Community Foundation maintained a mini-grant program to complement the work of the agency and expand participation to other community agencies interested in demonstrating new and innovative approaches to child care services and child care staff training.

Perhaps the agency had too much work, too little capital, and the burden of too heavy expectations in its first years. Despite capable board leadership, it struggled to find a sufficiently broad base of

Commitment

Resources

Skills

funding to support its focus on low-income families. When it sought funds by shifting focus to serve the business community, it lost United Way support. Finally in Year Four it restructured, refocused, restaffed, and found more solid footing. It convened two community task forces of business, civic, and child care leaders to make recommendations for a new mission and new four-point action plan. It reinstated low-income initiatives as primary, regained United Way support, won additional support from a mix of public and private sources, and regained the programmatic momentum it showed early when it was chosen as a national model by the Junior League.

Advocacy by Board and staff helped in passage of historic national child legislation that is to bring almost $50 million in child care block grant money into South Carolina for purposes complementary to the agency. It published and distributed a Directory of Children's Services. It expanded information and referral services. It helped local businesses develop child care options and services. It developed a buddy system pairing five low-income churches with five middle-income churches providing peer support, in-kind financial assistance, training and volunteers in child care efforts. It supported training programs for pre-service and in-service training of child care center personnel. And it kept the issue in front of the public through media exposure and conferences.

Greenville's Child continues reinvigorated well beyond the conclusion of the Program. Example: A $250,000 grant from the Greenville County Redevelopment Authority — its largest ever — is allowing it build a state-of-the-art child-development center to serve 200 preschool children in West Greenville's textile mill communities; the site was donated by a local business.

Commitment

Resources

Skills

Community Foundation of Greater Memphis
Tennessee

John K. Fockler, President (until mid-1989)
Gid H. Smith, President (since mid-1989)

The Community Foundation of Greater Memphis "will become the leading and most vital philanthropic organization in this area by serving donors, making grants, and engaging in community initiatives in order to have an increasingly beneficial effect on the quality of life of the people who live here."

In the first years of its Adolescent Pregnancy Prevention Initiative, applicant agencies to the Foundation's focused grantmaking program had to pass a strict litmus test: they were required to make the case that their efforts would "actually reduce the likelihood of a primary or secondary pregnancy." Using such a guideline assured the Foundation that scarce resources would not be spent in ways that diluted the Program's intentions.

Fifteen adolescent pregnancy prevention programs were funded during the five year period of the Program (just under $300,000). In the third year, the project's advisory committee decided to narrow the focus to previously funded agencies that have demonstrated the most effectiveness in preventing pregnancy.

An independent evaluation commissioned by the community foundation to study its Program's grantees found the same success factors that others have found (target adolescents early, target males and females, stay with them long-term, address not just pregnancy but a range of issues, check on your results). Grantees indicated that programs like theirs were gaining acceptance by city and county officials. Remember that in Memphis, recognition of adolescent pregnancy as a civic or community problem had not been embraced at the time the Foundation applied to the Program. Recognition of the problem by public officials and increasingly larger public constituencies was a significant advance in Memphis.

Agencies were brought together, first by the Community Foundation and later by the city and county Health Departments, for nonthreatening "brown bag lunches." These were important for finding common ground on a volatile and divisive issue.

Grants helped some organizations begin programs for which they gained local and national recognition. Others allowed local organizations to adopt recognized models promoted by national organizations. Most of the programs are being continued by the agencies without the community foundation's assistance.

Foundation officials cited several major impacts of their initiative. More groups are addressing adolescent pregnancy than before, and the media are paying more attention to the problem. Adolescent pregnancy is more viewed by the community as a community problem and not just a problem for adolescent parents and their children. The Foundation received considerable recognition for its efforts, and gained legitimacy in the African American community where many of the initiative's grants were made on recommendation of a diverse program advisory committee.

Commitment

Resources

Skills

Rochester Area Foundation
New York

Linda S. Weinstein, President (until 1993)
Jennifer Leonard, President (1993 —)

Commitment

Rochester Area Foundation is a "community-based endowment that matches the philanthropic interest of donors with unmet community needs. As a multi-county community foundation, RAF strives to enhance the quality of life for everyone through leadership and innovation in identifying and responding to the community's continuing and changing priorities."

Resources

A study commissioned early in the Foundation's early childhood education (ECE) initiative identified four areas for investment: improved quality of programs, increased quantity of programs, broadened options available to parents, and improved program accessibility. These findings were aired thoroughly among provider groups and the general public, and a Steering Committee was formed of ECE professionals and provider leaders. This group chose to focus on "increased quality," and chose further to adopt already accepted standards of quality, those passed by the National Association for the Education of Young Children (NAEYC).

Skills

By Year Three, when a crisis in public funding made it obvious that heavier hitters would be needed to move the Steering Committee's agenda and make something happen, the Foundation had become publicly viable and visible enough to prevail upon the Mayor to convene a new Sponsors' Group of the area's biggest funders. This Sponsors' Group became a highly successful collaboration of the City, County, United Way, two business groups, Rochester Grantmakers Forum, and the Foundation, with about $400,000/year at the table and a "total quality" process assertively chaired by a top Xerox retiree.

Early focus on program quality resulted in community adoption of the National Association for the Education of Young Children's standards, followed by an increase in local NAEYC accredited centers from three in 1990 to 20 by the end of 1993. The Foundation assisted in formation of a donors' group that provides funds for weaker programs to meet quality standards. Training opportunities were opened to subsidize low-income teachers and aides to gain Child Development Associate certification. Efforts to expand the number of children served resulted in adding more than 1000 new slots in child care centers and family day care homes. Large and small corporations have partnered with the school district in novel Family Learning Centers. Private donors are responsible for at least 350 additional children served.

The strategy is updated every year. Goals have been consistent throughout, continuing well past the Foundation's participation in the Leadership Program. Priorities are adjusted as accomplishments in one area allow for expanding investment in others.

Commitment

Resources

Skills

Community Foundation for Southeastern Michigan
Detroit

Mariam C. Noland, President

The Community Foundation for Southeastern Michigan is "a unique charitable organization built by donors concerned about the welfare of our [seven-county] region . . . Together, we are creating 'community capital,' a permanent charitable endowment that will benefit our region now and for generations to come. A Board of 45 distinguished local citizens oversees this endowment and distributes its income in grants for urgent community needs."

Project Prevention was designed "to inform and motivate community leaders, increase the region's commitment to substance abuse prevention, and develop effective long-term prevention strategies that will work in southeastern Michigan." "Prevention" in the field of substance abuse as well as most other social problem areas typically is funded to a much lesser extent than "treatment" or, in this arena, law enforcement. The community foundation wanted to legitimize "prevention" on the pretext that an ounce of prevention is worth a pound of cure, and a stitch in time saves nine.

First step: convene a group of representatives from industry, labor, government, the media, religious congregations, and civic groups from the seven southeastern Michigan counties. They built a prevention-friendly network for themselves and the Foundation.

Next: assemble quality information on high-yield prevention strategies and make it available to the community as an aid to problem solving. To do this, the community foundation (with the additional support of The Skillman Foundation) commissioned the University of Michigan's School of Public Health to organize "think tank" sessions of scholars, expert practitioners and civic leaders to bring together the best information on prevention strategies that could serve the region. The School produced "Action Strategies for Preventing Substance Abuse: A Resource Manual for Southeastern Michigan," and the Foundation distributed it to over 600+ entities in its region. A major regional conference was held as the culmination of the Think Tank's work to educate local policy makers and practitioners of promising substance abuse prevention models available to them.

Finally: invest in projects that promise to demonstrate the merits of the models and principles just unveiled. Using a Request for Proposals procedure and pre-grant training workshops, the Foundation noticed more thoughtful discussion of the issues, and a substantial increase in proposal quality than it was used to in proposals received "over the transom." Over $400,000 was distributed to 15 organizations.

While public policy was not obviously affected and public funding has precipitously dropped, there are some indications that programs have made prevention principles more central to their efforts.

As a final act of community education, the Foundation produced and distributed over 5,000 copies of a highly informative and presentable summary, "Preventing Substance Abuse: Strategies and Findings from Project Prevention, 1987-1991." The Foundation then secured a $500,000 endowment from the Ford Motor Company, to support the Foundation's interest in substance abuse prevention permanently.

Commitment

Resources

Skills

Baltimore Community Foundation
Maryland

Eugene Struckhoff, President (until 1990)
Timothy Armbruster, President (1990 —)

The Baltimore Community Foundation "uses both traditional and non-traditional forms of collaboration to coordinate and focus existing resources, educate the public and its elected representatives about community problems, and attract charitable dollars from individuals and private institutions, both local and national."

Through its Children and Families Initiative, the Foundation seeks to galvanize political and public will to invest in areas that improve the outlook for all children, especially those who are disadvantaged. Most of the Foundation's grantmaking and convening work has been to: (a) broaden and strengthen the constituency for children; (b) encourage early investment and prevention; and (c) build and support partnerships (parents, teachers, business, nonprofit youth agencies, youth, schools, public agencies) which provide the support, at the school and neighborhood level, which youth need to succeed, academically and socially.

One centerpiece project has been "Ready At Five," in which the Foundation is a partner and funder. A formally structured coalition of the most significant networks of seniors, business councils, and pediatricians, it works with advocates on early investment in children and supports public and private programs and policies which invest early in the health and welfare of children 0 to 5 years old. Activities include directing a campaign for improved kids' TV; increasing participation in Head Start and WIC; initiating a statewide effort to increase the number of children who are fully immunized by age 2; and conducting statewide public education campaigns. Ready at Five has received additional funding from the State Office of Children, Youth and Families, the National Coalition of Community Foundations for Youth, and several local corporations and foundations.

Another is the Dunbar Project, focusing on one inner-city neighborhood in Baltimore, designed formally as a partnership of
parents, teachers, principals, business, Hopkins Hospital, public
agencies, and nonprofit groups to connect health and human
services with three elementary and two middle schools. A public/
private Coordinating Council identifies needs, assess current resources, and develops plans to augment and deploy those
resources.

Still other efforts focus on educating business, civic, and political
leadership about the problems of children in Maryland, and on collecting data and publishing an annual report card on the state of
Maryland's children. Still another recruits parents to advocate for
family-friendly business and public policies in central Maryland.

In the first four years of the Children and Families Initiative, the
Foundation granted $1.2 million to support services and advocacy
for children and families, a little over half in 1992 alone to 26 different projects. The Foundation's $1 million investment, its conven-
ing and work in partnerships, leveraged over $2 million from local
and national funders for children's programs.

The Foundation leveraged the Ford opportunity and money to
attract other large institutional money and the participation of significant institutional partners. This initiative will clearly endure beyond the life of the Ford money, well embedded within the
community foundation.

Commitment

Resources

Skills

Community Foundation for Greater Lorain County
Lorain, Ohio

Carol G. Simonetti, Executive Director

"The Community Foundation of Greater Lorain County exists: to mobilize individuals to become active partners in building a better community; to provide a permanent instrument for receiving and managing charitable gifts and bequests; to support innovative programs and act as a catalyst in identifying problems and sharing information with individuals, other foundations, corporations and organizations; and to exercise and promote leadership in meeting the changing needs and opportunities in the community. Through these efforts the Foundation seeks to improve the quality of life and to instill a greater sense of unity in the Greater Lorain County community."

In planning its education initiative, the community foundation noted that public confidence in the county's public schools was low, and that the county's distinct regions were disunited and disparate in their approach to education, with fifteen separate school districts. It saw an opportunity to counteract a dysfunctional system by giving the public a neutral county-wide vehicle for mobilizing interest and creating change in the public school system.

In a major public effort, the Foundation conducted focus groups of concerned parents throughout the county, commissioned a major survey, then held public hearings — all to give people a chance to express themselves, suggest solutions, and group themselves around the issue. The primary recommendation: continue to play the county-wide catalytic role, and "create change without becoming part of the bureaucracy." Three major lines of development emerged.

The centerpiece is the creation, in the fifth year of the initiative, of the Center for Leadership in Education that focuses intensively on the continuing education and professional development of the principal stakeholders involved in public education — teachers and administrators, superintendents and boards, parents, business and labor, government, and concerned community organizations. Creation of this center followed a capacity assessment of the community sponsored by the business leadership and done by the evaluator for the original model of this Center in Louisville, Kentucky, and several site visits to Louisville by the educational and business leadership of the county.

Second, the community foundation created a "Great Ideas for Education" small grants program "to encourage innovation, achievement, parental involvement and higher expectations."

The third major accomplishment is the creation of school endowments in each of the school districts in Lorain County, each affiliated with the Foundation. With a balance of $314,000 when it began in the Leadership Program, these school district endowments had reached $2 million when it ended. These endowments were stimulated with a $25,000 challenge grant given by the local Nord Family Foundation, to be matched dollar-for-dollar by gifts from individuals, businesses, or organizations wishing to support their particular school district. The Nord grant emphasizes projects which promote team building within individual schools, where "team" includes building administrators, teachers, students, and parents.

Commitment

Resources

Skills

Madison Community Foundation
Wisconsin

Jane T. Coleman, Executive Director

Commitment

"The Madison Community Foundation secures, manages and distributes philanthropic contributions for a varied group of donors in the Madison/Dane County area. We strive to be responsive to donor interests by providing a flexible and prudently managed means to direct their charitable assets to the community's greatest benefit. Madison Community Foundation works with other foundations, corporations and organizations to identify community assets and innovative ways to build on community strengths. The Foundation also encourages participation by the community's civic, corporate and philanthropic leaders . . ."

Resources

The Madison Community Foundation wanted to design an initiative to help minimize school dropouts by reducing the risks for "at risk" children. Most important, it wanted to show this could be done by getting more from existing resources than from creating a new agency. It compromised: the community foundation created Project Opportunity, an "arrangement" in which the Foundation coordinates rather than provides services (or have another agency provide services) for sixteen grade school children and their families. The Foundation will stay with them to high school graduation and help them go on to college or employment. Services are provided through an unusual and experimental combination of nontraditional resources. The Foundation supplies a project manager who facilitates access to services for these kids and their families.

Skills

Examples: A leading Presbyterian church helped begin the project by guaranteeing a specified amount of post secondary tuition for the sixteen students. An African American church provides mentors. Mentoring became so popular it quickly grew beyond these two churches, and beyond these sixteen kids; a city-wide mentoring and tutoring network is developing through the leadership of Madison Community Foundation volunteers, and then through Madison Community Foundation support to a city-wide coalition of churches. The benefits of mentoring go not just to the students, but to the mentors themselves; mentoring allows a wide variety of people to become directly involved in contributing to one solution to modern difficulties in public education. Staff, mentors, and tutors support the kids and their families in different areas of school work, and in "success skills": self-esteem, wellness, self-motivation, taking responsibility, decision-making, communicating, etc.

Several other agencies and organizations have, at different times, provided services to the participants in the program, but the mentoring networks have been the most enduring. The Foundation has extended Project Opportunity for two additional years, taking it to the time participants can graduate from high school. Foundation staff have become deeply immersed and knowledgeable in the difficulties of urban public education, and look for ways to use this knowledge productively. A final evaluation of the project will seek to document what Project Opportunity has in fact demonstrated.

Commitment

Resources

Skills

Greater New Orleans Foundation
Louisiana

Patricia C. Mason, Executive Director (until 1992)
Gregory Ben Johnson, Executive Director (1992 —)

Commitment

The Greater New Orleans Foundation "improves the quality of life for all citizens of our area, now and for future generations. As a catalyst and resource for philanthropy we build permanent endowments for our community's changing issues and opportunities; demonstrate strategic grantmaking which invests in leaders and systemic change; and serve as a flexible and cost-effective vehicle for philanthropists to invest in their community."

Resources

Operating the first two years as "The Adolescent/Teen Pregnancy Prevention Project" the Foundation's initiative focused on being of service to segments of the community that were underserved by existing programs. Advised by a Steering Committee that developed consensus-based guidelines for grantmaking, it called on an expanded cast of characters, reaching broadly into the communities most immediately affected by the problem, notably the African-American community. During this period the Foundation (a) funded a citizen's dialogue, neighborhood by neighborhood, entitled "Let's Talk." This dialogue allowed ordinary citizens to discuss teenage pregnancy, its genesis and its results; (b) funded seven pilot programs which addressed the twin goals of enhancing the ability of economically disadvantaged youth in decision making skills, and supporting services for pregnant or parenting teens.

Skills

The Foundation then broadened its initiative, renaming it "Youth: Opportunities and Options," and expanding its scope to include "prevention" in all areas affecting youth. This expansion builds on the premise that teen pregnancy is a symptom of a larger problem, and one must build on existing assets to support youth opportunities and options in the community.

The Foundation kept, however, its wish to connect with grassroots groups and minority organizations that other foundations typically do not see, and made a conscious effort to model strategies of inclusiveness with the Foundation's own staff, committees, and Board. The minority community, we heard from more than one prominent spokesperson, "feels like a part of the process."

The Foundation sought to relate and partner with other local funders, beginning with funding the New Orleans Council for Children, a collaborative of 60+ human service agencies, business and civic leaders focused on establishing a coordinated system of services of children age zero to five. Other funders have followed the Foundation in providing seed grants and start-up costs to high quality social and youth development programs. The largest corporation in the state, Freeport-McMoran, created a complementary Recreational Trust fund with $500,000.

The Distribution Committee seeks out groups that "maximize commitment, resources, and problem-solving responses," deliberately seeking to build capacity in the nonprofit arena serving youth. The Youth: Opportunities and Options program is complemented by an Environmental Program and an Affordable Housing and Neighborhood Revitalization Program.

Commitment

Resources

Skills

Central New York Community Foundation
Syracuse

Margaret G. Ogden, President

The mission of the Central New York Community Foundation is "to identify and initiate effective, creative actions which enrich the community by receiving, managing and disbursing charitable funds. It does this by encouraging the growth of the community foundation's permanent endowment; by providing a vehicle for donations from individuals, families, corporations and organizations with varied interests; by evaluating and addressing emerging and changing community needs; by serving as a neutral leader to stimulate and coordinate actions among various organizations to accomplish common objectives; and by making grants which are consistent with the above."

From the outset, the Child Care Project convened a diverse community leadership to identify child care issues. It met four times a year, set priorities and made recommendations to the Foundation board for grants for the Project. This involvement of business, public and private sector, not-for-profit agency staff and child care providers helped create a greater awareness and commitment in those sectors to resolving some of the community's child care problems.

In a state where child care is high on the public agenda, with more public monies and more enlightened public policy than in most states, the community foundation recognized its role was different than the public sector's. The public sector was to take care of the structure, availability, and cost of child care, but the commu-

Commitment

Resources

Skills

nity foundation decided it could play a useful role in improving the service quality of the child care industry. After more than a year of self-education, the Advisory Committee decided that training should become the major focus, and formulated five major training recommendations to develop a variety of training and assistance programs for people who take care of young children for a living.

Three of these recommendations were addressed in the remaining years of the initiative by supporting several dozen low-income day care providers in attaining the Child Development Associate certificate, by providing on site technical assistance at child care centers that helped them meet accreditation, by supporting low income individuals to attend courses, seminars, and workshops, by funding a Risk Management Course for 30 child care center directors and board members, by providing funding for a conference called "Family Policies That Work At Work," by supporting the creation of the Family Day Care association, by supporting the County Child Care Council (which will replicate the Risk Management Course in other counties in the state), and by providing support for the Annual Legislative Breakfast to inform city, county, and state lawmakers about the Child Care Legislative Agenda. This type of advocacy encouraged the child care community to speak out for higher wages, market rates, and increased support. For these efforts to improve the quality of local child care, the Community Foundation was awarded the "Decade of the Child Award" by the state's first lady.

Commitment

Resources

Skills

Foundation Northwest, The Community Foundation
Spokane, Washington

Jeanne L. Ager, Executive Director (until mid 1990)
Peter A. Jackson, President (1991 —)

Commitment

"Foundation Northwest, The Community Foundation, is a permanent endowment for the community, built by gifts from individuals, families and organizations committed to meeting the changing needs of the Inland Northwest."

But it was the Spokane Inland Northwest Community Foundation that originally entered the Leadership Program, with an initiative called Project Self-Sufficiency, which in turn was little more than a Federally-funded agency intending to help mothers on welfare remove themselves from those rolls and that lifestyle.

Resources

Faltering in its efforts to take full advantage of the opportunities created by the Leadership Program, the Board hired a new executive director towards the end of the second year, refreshed its own leadership and outlook, and created a new name, new logo, new corporate form, and new operating and grantmaking philosophies.

Skills

While the original agency sponsoring Project Self-Sufficiency was given financial support to expand its base, plan ahead, revitalize itself and ultimately find a new home at the Community College, the Foundation designed a new program meant primarily to support the management abilities of a whole range of family-serving agencies operating in the region. Called ManagementWorks! it provides technical assistance to agencies whose mission is to improve the quality of life for low income women with dependent children. The goal is to enhance the long-term capacity of an organization to serve its clients.

The grants program has provided funding for agencies to undertake a rigorous self-assessment process, then shop for a consultant to develop a workplan and facilitate progress through it. The consultant is accountable to the agency. The program is designed to support strategic planning, board development, financial management, volunteer recruiting and training, fundraising and other aspects of nonprofit organization management; most requests have been for strategic planning. These kinds of activities are exactly the kind that are so hard to find funds for; the money needed for agencies to plan or develop their skills, much less to reinvent themselves, is typically not contained in the public budgets that tend to support these organizations.

Initially few organizations applied, so the Foundation commissioned a survey of target agencies which identified fears and barriers to using technical assistance or to applying for support. Now the biggest problem is a shortage of consultants in the region. The Foundation has expanded the program to address the management concerns of other areas — in arts, for example — by supplementing the project fund from its discretionary funds. The Foundation hopes to continue the program with funds raised specially for that purpose.

Commitment

Resources

Skills

The Community Foundation Serving Richmond and Central Virginia

Richmond

Darcy S. Oman, President

Commitment

This community foundation (formerly the Greater Richmond Community Foundation) "seeks to provide effective stewardship of philanthropic assets entrusted to the Foundation's care by donors who wish to benefit or enhance the quality of community life." A primary purpose is "to exercise leadership in the philanthropic community by designing innovative programs and acting as a catalyst in the identification and sharing of information with others about important community problems and opportunities."

Resources

This Foundation's Neighborhoods Grants Initiative began as a five-year program commitment designed to strengthen low- and low/moderate income neighborhoods by supporting resident-based initiatives. The program, supported by grant monies from the Leadership Program and by other discretionary funds held by the Foundation, focused on two objectives: (1) to develop the capacity of low- and low/moderate income neighborhood groups to identify, influence, and resolve local problems; and (2) to serve as a catalyst for increasing the supply of decent, affordable neighborhood-based housing in metropolitan Richmond.

Skills

The Foundation's grants list reveals, as does feedback with the Foundation's grantees, that emphasis was put on finding the best use of scarce monies — uses that other funders could not support. Midway through the initiative, the Local Initiatives Support Corporation (LISC), which specializes in amassing capital for the bricks-and-mortar aspects of neighborhood-based housing development, set up shop in Richmond. This allowed the Foundation to deploy money in ways that complement LISC's so that together they do the most good in the highly technical field of housing development. These include start-up money, predevelopment money, money for organizing the human resources of a neighborhood; in short, staking emerging groups and organizations to development resources that could not be obtained from LISC and public sector programs.

In the beginning of the initiative, the Foundation specialized in project grants, but midway through it increased its emphasis on capacity-building strategies; these allowed technical assistance services to go to neighborhood organizations and neighborhood-based community development corporations. These funds were used to support intensive technical assistance and/or specialized training needs which were beyond the skills and capacity of community foundation staff; to encourage resource sharing and dialogue among community and neighborhood leaders; and, to support public education efforts sponsored by the Foundation around affordable housing neighborhood issues. These are all activities that neighborhood revitalization and nonprofit housing efforts find hardest to fund, and serve to strengthen in a more enduring way the capacity of groups working in the field of neighborhood revitalization.

In the initiative's last year the Foundation restructured its discretionary grantmaking into three program initiatives which encompass the majority of the Foundation's discretionary giving. The Neighborhoods Grants Initiative is to be carried forward under the larger rubric of "Strengthening Families — Strengthening Communities," its largest discretionary program. This initiative has four major funding priorities: projects which enable children to overcome the effects of poverty; promote families' independence from public assistance; encourage neighborhoods to resolve local problems; and enrich family and community life.

Commitment

Resources

Skills

East Tennessee Foundation
Knoxville

Katharine K. Pearson, Executive Director

The East Tennessee Foundation, while based in Knoxville, serves 18 counties of East Tennessee. Its mission is "to enrich the quality of life in our area by bringing together donors and community organizations in partnerships that are responsive to specific opportunities and needs — both present and future. We serve East Tennessee by building a permanent pool of endowments and making grants to programs and projects that we believe will best serve this region and its people."

The Youth Endowment was created in 1987 as part of an effort supported by the US Department of Health and Human Services, to serve as "a perpetual source of funds to be used in addressing problems and issues affecting young people in East Tennessee. The fund's primary goal is to develop creative solutions to the problems facing at-risk children and youth in our region."

While the goal of its Youth Initiative is simply stated, its strength is in the way themes of community development and regionalism are woven into the grants list. While focusing on youth, the grants list reflects a concern with rural development, leadership development, rural health, economic development, neighborhood revitalization, nonprofit infrastructure development, and voluntarism in lieu of professionalized social services. Collaboration among nonprofit applicants is stressed in the guidelines, as is "a commitment to involve community members in program development."

Midway through the initiative, the Foundation added to its program of project support to include "Grants for Excellence" to outstanding area agencies and youth organizations. "Above and Beyond Awards" are presented every other year at a well-attended dinner and awards ceremony to outstanding professionals in service to children and families in East Tennessee. This move was

Commitment

Resources

Skills

predicated on the following rationale that emerged from the Foundation's discussions and evaluations of the previous three years: (a) partnerships are often effective in leveraging resources and creating innovative programs; (b) many organizations welcome the idea of long-term, multi-faceted programs; (c) those agencies or youth groups that are outstanding in some way should be recognized and supported; (d) problems of at-risk youth are complex and interrelated, and therefore effective solutions must recognize and address this reality.

This Foundation's grantmaking stands out particularly in the way it is strengthening the infrastructure in the tough conditions of its region. Grantees praised them for inducing productive partnerships and collaborations, without the "us/them" feeling that often creeps into funder/grantee relationships. Instead the Foundation positions itself more as an "ally," in which the Foundation is the funding partner and the nonprofits do the work.

Also helping to support this position are these features of the Foundation's activities: the more focused grantmaking guidelines; technical assistance provided to applicants and grantees; convening groups of grantees in the Youth initiative that typically have not had any other mechanism for meeting each other. One particularly strong project was staked to a few hundred dollars to share its projects with other counties in the region. Remember that a tradition of isolation and independence, along with a dearth of hard capital, are two critical context factors that impede progress in the region.

Because of its good track record with the Youth Endowment, East Tennessee Foundation has become a funding partner with several local foundations and corporations.

Commitment

Resources

Skills

Greater Triangle Community Foundation
Research Triangle Park, North Carolina

Shannon E. St. John, Executive Director

The mission of this foundation is "to expand private philanthropy in the Triangle area, including the communities of Wake, Durham, and Orange Counties. The Foundation accomplishes its mission by targeting charitable grants toward the community's most pressing needs and promising opportunities, and by carefully managing a wide variety of philanthropic funds for individuals, corporations, and charitable agencies."

Its Regionalism initiative was built on the premise that regional cooperative planning and action is necessary to preserve and enhance the Triangle's economic vitality and quality of life, and was designed to promote and support regional cooperation among the three counties.

A study completed by the Foundation, "Philanthropy in the Triangle," pointed the way for many later initiative activities. In a first-ever study of the region's 1200 nonprofits, it aimed at promoting a greater level of understanding of the role, structure, and financial support of the Triangle's nonprofit sector. The study found that the nonprofit sector is a very significant social and economic force in the region, but is "surprisingly dependent upon government funding as a source of revenue." The study produced a number of recommendations aimed at strengthening and making more vital the region's nonprofit sector, some of which the Foundation implemented during the life of the initiative.

Regional Roundtables brought together nonprofit leaders, state or local policy makers, academic researchers, local corporate or individual donors, elected or appointed officials and other concerned community volunteers from across county lines to discuss an area of particular importance or concern in the Triangle. Roundtables were convened on the issues of "Human Services and Client Transportation," "Affordable and Accessible Child-Care," and "Affordable Housing Alternatives in the Triangle," topics discovered in the above study as critical to the vitality of the region.

Nine "regional community grants" totaling $137,320 were made to support "new initiatives or special projects which promote new forms of cooperation, coordination of services or activities, resource sharing, and mutual responsibility across the Triangle area counties."

Leadership Triangle brings together a select group of young leaders who were already active in their communities. The program has three goals: to educate participants on the most pressing issues, challenges, and opportunities facing the region; to further develop the participants' skills that enhance their ability to lead within their communities and the region; and to develop an ongoing network of leaders who have the skills, interest, and commitment to continue working for the betterment of the region.

Leadership Triangle graduates decided to take the money earmarked for a special project and reinvest it in strengthening the next cycle of Leadership Triangle, saying that a critical mass of alumnae was needed to make a difference, and that participants need good support to act on what they've learned.

The theme of "regionalism" allowed the Foundation to bring people together, induce discussion on critical issues, catalyze cooperation, encourage networking and coalition building, coordinate training, develop broader-based leadership, and otherwise promote and begin to implement a regional vision for the area.

Commitment

Resources

Skills

185

Tucson Community Foundation
Arizona

Donna L. Grant, Executive Director

The mission of the Tucson Community Foundation is "to stimulate philanthropic resources and create a healthy, productive community in Southern Arizona. In order to accomplish the stated mission, the Foundation will: create and manage permanent endowments; serve as catalyst and convener to identify community needs; encourage collaborative approaches to address community needs; promote solutions which confront the root causes of problems, with special emphasis on empowering the disadvantaged and the underserved; stimulate innovative projects and programs that address emerging or unmet needs; reflect the diversity of our community in the foundation's planning, decision-making, and grantmaking; and respect individual concerns of citizens while striving for community consensus."

The Tucson Community Foundation began its children's endowment when it entered into a cooperative arrangement with the Arizona Community Foundation (a Round One participant in this Program, based in Phoenix) to create the Children's Trust Fund. Two years later, when Tucson joined the Leadership Program, Tucson Community Foundation created its own program initiative to support children's mental illness prevention efforts within Pima County. After allying with the Mayor's Task Force for Children, the Foundation commissioned a needs assessment to discover where to focus its scarce resource. The study plotted areas of high problem prevalence and areas with few resources in the form of institu-

Commitment

Resources

Skills

tionalized services. That map, coupled with a guidebook produced by Arizona State University on the essential ingredients required to make prevention efforts work, guided the Foundation to likely locales and good prospects for grant support.

Three complementary streams emerged. First was the development of a Family Resource Center, sited in an area that allows it to collaborate with three adjoining neighborhood groups also supported by the Foundation. The Center, along with other projects supported by the Foundation, strives to incorporate principles of "asset-based" programming, which rewards groups and individuals working to build on their strengths rather than reward them for "counting scars" or focusing on what's wrong with people. The second piece was to commit an entire round of discretionary grant dollars to prevention and early intervention efforts in areas targeted by the study mentioned above. The third is to commit $100,000 in support of groups or programs that can support the Family Resource Center with adjunct services.

The Tucson Community Foundation, along with the Arizona Community Foundation, form the Partnership for Children, "the nation's first statewide system reform initiative for children to emanate exclusively from within the private sector," funded also by the Ford Foundation.

Commitment

Resources

Skills

Chapter Seven

Conclusions, Critique, and Implications

In this chapter, we provide a detailed description of participants' progress — their growth and their limits to growth. Our analysis follows the 12-part framework of community foundation capacity introduced in Chapter Two. We then explain why this Program was so successful, and how its key features can probably be helpful in *any* program of support. Two sets of implications are then developed: one for community groups working to develop their *own* capacity and another for institutions wishing to help *other* community groups build capacity. We then revisit the three specific purposes of this book, and summarize the major lessons for communities.

Growth in capacity: A summary of participant development

The two major objectives of the Leadership Program for Community Foundations were achieved for virtually all participants: their discretionary financial resources increased, as did their community leadership skills[1]. As a major by-product, their organizational commitment increased and administrative infrastructures were strengthened.

These advances did not occur equally in all foundations. In some, resource development outstripped leadership development; in others, the reverse was true. In some, resource development was extraordinary, and in others only ordinary; the same can be said about leadership skill development. In a few, a strengthened administrative infrastructure was the primary legacy. Some grew rapidly in the first two years and then leveled off, while others were late bloomers. This pattern could be different: some shone early in resource development and late in leadership, and for others, the reverse was true.

---

1 Some readers may be dismayed at the lack of numbers in statements using "virtually all" or "some." I have tried throughout this book to stay consistent with the following usage, given a collection of eighteen community foundations.

"Virtually all"	All but 1-2
"Most"	More than 9
"Many", "several"	4-9
"Some", "a few"	1-3

This variation was expected and never deemed unhealthy by the Program's sponsors. A basic premise of the Program's design was that there was no "one best way" to build a community foundation, and no "one best profile" of success or effectiveness. This premise was amply borne out, from Day One. Indeed, it was obvious even in the applications.

Participants experienced some degree of growth in all 12 aspects of organizational life shown in Table 7-1. All participants also experienced limits to growth and difficulties in growing. Sometimes these difficulties were temporary, sometimes for longer periods.

The fundamental outcome intended by the Program's sponsors and then achieved by participants, was "increased capacity," which was broken down into four major areas:

- organizational development;

- financial resource development;

- community leadership;

- grantmaking and programming.

These can be further broken into the 12 areas summarized in Table 7-1, and elaborated in Chapters Three, Four, and Five.

Note that some areas of this catalog of outcomes relate to "taking on capacity" and some to "giving off capacity." The classification in Table 7-1 reflects the prevailing emphasis during the earliest days of the Program (notably the requirements of making the match and launching an initiative) better than those that became dominant in its last two years (notably long-term resource development and managing the end of an initiative). Nevertheless, a summary using the framework the participants used throughout the Program to document progress can be helpful. Because the Program's sponsors wanted this synthesis to be made available before the experience of Rounds One and Two became outdated, Round Three participants were at most only mid-way through their five-year program during the development of this book. The results reported in Table 7-1 speak only to the experience of Rounds One and Two.

Table 7-1

Summary of progress in 12 key areas of capacity building

A. Organizational development

1. Board

Growth: Virtually all boards functioned increasingly as policy makers for operations, as ambassadors for the institution, as providers of access to resources, and as providers of diverse community perspectives.

Limits and difficulties: Almost all executive directors wished their boards would do even more, especially with regard to financial resource development. A genuinely productive relationship between executives and board leadership was often difficult to create or sustain because of limited terms.

2. Staff

Growth: Staffing grew in number and specialization, with enhanced skills that directly enabled the foundation to act in accordance with its mission statement.

Limits and difficulties: Organizational growth was stressful, particularly on staff who had to do more and more until additional staff members were hired. Issues of growth tested the human resource management abilities of the executive director. Turnover in the executive position had unpredictable effects on the growth of the foundation: some flourished, others struggled.

3. Administration

Growth: Participating community foundations increasingly operated by policy created by board/staff cooperation and driven by pursuit of mission and principles of service. Foundation staff showed great flair for increased sophistication of operation without becoming correspondingly bureaucratic, inflexible, or timid.

Limits and difficulties: The diversity represented on participants' grant lists and on foundation advisory committees grew substantially faster than the diversity of foundation board, staff, and donor base. Genuine success in diversification — getting beyond "headcounts" to experiencing enhanced capabilities and credibility as a broad-based community institution — was only occasional.

B. Financial resource development

4. Endowment growth

Growth: Virtually all participants substantially increased their permanent endowment and the proportion of discretionary endowment. In doing so, they improved their skills in two major strategies of financial resource development: asking directly for discretionary funds that satisfied a match requirement and cultivating prospects for estate planning that form the basis for long-term endowment growth.

Limits and difficulties: Returning to the rigors of long-term financial resource growth did not happen for most participants until taking at least a year as a "break," after making the match. Even then, it proved difficult for many to find the time or energy to formulate, fund, and act on long-term growth strategies.

5. Communications

Growth: All participants increased their visibility in appropriate segments of the community by creating materials that communicated the roles of community philanthropy.

Limits and difficulties: Getting out the story of the community foundation to pertinent segments of the community is a time-consuming job. It required almost one half-time person's attention in the faster-growing community foundation participants. Getting salary support for that person was not easy.

6. Administrative support

Growth: Participants raised revenues to support operations, increasing resources in ways that sustained growth on a reasonably steady and manageable course. Investment portfolios were managed with increasing professionalism.

Limits and difficulties: There were so many more opportunities for foundation growth and service than could be supported by most administrative budgets, especially those that relied only on internal sources of support. Funding long-term growth was virtually impossible without outside support.

C. Community leadership

7. Leadership skills

Growth: Participants increased their skills in the roles a community foundation can play in addressing a community issue. Most developed their convening and advisory group leadership skills to a high level. Most became more practiced in the "catalytic" style.

Limits and difficulties: Most foundations reported at least one blunder in convening — an incomplete guest list, ambivalence in limits to authority, moving from talk to action, or closing out the group's work.

8. Contributions to progress in a community initiative

Growth: Participants successfully increased the legitimacy, focus, momentum, and support that their communities gave to addressing their chosen issue.

Limits and difficulties: Becoming more successful and visible created expectations in the community that were difficult to meet, especially when resources did not grow as quickly as wished.

9. Institutional linkages

Growth: Virtually all participants strengthened their relationships with different segments of the community, especially city, county, and regional governments; non-traditional and racial/ethnic minority organizations; coalitions and associations; and advocacy groups. Most also helped to strengthen relationships *among* those different segments.

Limits and difficulties: A small number of participants discovered that one risk of "taking leadership" is inadvertently taking leadership from another group which is already playing a valuable role.

D. Grantmaking and programming

10. Grantmaking procedures

Growth: Participants strengthened their procedures for discretionary grantmaking, basing their decisions more on developed priorities and guidelines.

Limits and difficulties: Distribution committees struggled with questions of continuity and scale: What warrants a decision to fund for a second year? Should we make larger or smaller grants? It was a rare committee, however, that based such decisions on knowledge of lessons learned from recent grantmaking.

11. Strategic grantmaking

Growth: All participants developed a portfolio of grants or projects conducive to building the community's capacity to make gains in the foundation's chosen issue area.

Limits and difficulties: While all participants grew in capacity and benefited from the capacity-inducing features of this Program, few systematically incorporated these same features into their own programming so that their grantees could build *their* capacity.

12. Programming effectiveness

Growth: Most participants strengthened their approach to other issues in the community by drawing on the experience gained from this community initiative.

Limits and difficulties: Keeping the momentum of successful efforts going, so that they have a healthy future inside or outside the foundation, was a major challenge.

This Program accomplished its goals for virtually all participants: increased discretionary resources and increased community leadership skills. Virtually all participants achieved the next level of growth — oftentimes the next several levels — in these two areas, as well as in the overall category of "organizational capacity." All have attained a substantial degree of greater usefulness to their communities. Now, after five years of participation, most can glimpse the challenges at the next levels: the sustained incorporation of long-term resource development strategies and the systematic inclusion of capacity-inducing features into their own programming and grantmaking so that *other* community groups benefit.

Why the Program worked:
Its capacity building features

The results of this Program have been impressive; participants have grown significantly in capacity. Their own commitment, resources, and skills have been greatly enhanced. While this growth was often stressful, all participants rated the experience to be a significant net gain for their institutions.

Much of the success of this Program can be attributed directly to its design and implementation. All of its features, if closely examined, can be seen to contribute directly to gains in community foundation capacity. If they contribute to the capacity of community foundations, chances are these features, if designed into other grantmaking programs, could contribute to the capacity of other kinds of community groups as well.

Here, the Program's features are critiqued in two major categories: the design or architecture of the Program itself and the package of managed support for participants.

Architecture of the Program

Capacity building theme. The overriding goal of the Program and its consistent message to participants was, "Build your capacity." Virtually all decisions in program design and implementation were weighed against this purpose.

For example, the choice of a foundation's community initiative — early childhood education, affordable housing, or another area — mattered little to the Ford Foundation as applicants were screened. What mattered was whether the applicant could make the case that taking on its proposed initiative would produce an enduring gain for the foundation in its capacity to be of future service to the community.

Incentive to increase discretionary financial resources. A principal barrier keeping community foundations from playing a useful leadership role was their relative lack of discretionary financial resources. The Program sponsors addressed this by creating a goal ("raise $1 million in new permanent discretionary funds") plus an incentive ("we'll give you $500,000 when you do") to raise such resources: a two-for-one match, which all participants met by the required deadline. Participating community foundations gained the practice and nerve to "make the ask" for this rare kind of resource after mobilizing the board, rehearsing the case, and working up the courage to do so.

While undertaking concerted efforts to raise this type of money in the short term actually distracted several participants momentarily from long-term efforts, the result was uniformly positive. Infrastructures were shored up, and the organization was strengthened and positioned to better undertake the long-term efforts.

Encouragement to play a leadership role. Perhaps it was the Ford imprimatur, the realization that "our time is now," or the opportunity to follow through with momentum generated by the foundation's earlier work; in any case, official encouragement to play a leadership role genuinely emboldened participants in new ways.

All participants were acknowledged by these interviews to have become "much more of a community leader" in helping the community. While one can argue whether this meets or falls somewhat short of the official goal, to "help the community make progress in a significant problem area," all participants were credited with making progress in three key outcome areas: increasing or mobilizing community commitment, increasing community resources, and strengthening community building skills. Many participants came to recognize that these outcome areas were legitimate accomplishments for the leadership work of a community foundation — more legitimate, for example, than reduced teen pregnancy rates or even additional affordable housing stock — outcomes that occur far downstream of direct community foundation influence.

Combining financial resource development with community leadership. An unexpected but significant benefit of the Program was the symbiotic way in which financial resource development and community leadership development worked together to form an upward spiral of growth. Success with discretionary financial resource development allowed highly-visible programming. This programming led to new financial resources, and new leadership opportunities, and so on.

This dynamic was very powerful. Working on programming allowed the foundation to become skillful in programming; working on financial resource development allowed the foundation to become skillful in financial resource development. Working on both in the name of the larger purpose of institutional capacity building enhanced the growth-engendering power of each.

On the down side, the board became more versed in the skills of financial resource development and institution building than in the skills gained through the community initiative; those skills were developed almost exclusively by program staff. If key program staff leave, there will not be the capacity for creating successful community initiatives as much as there will be for financial resource development and institution building.

Support for administration of new efforts. Of the $100,000 granted each year to participants, at least $50,000 was distributed by participating community foundations in grants, but as much as $50,000 could be used to support their efforts.

Typically this was used to support a program officer and underwrite the costs of convening and hosting meetings. This general support gave most participants the breathing room required to expand their efforts on both the financial resource development and leadership development fronts; it was universally acknowledged to be a critical piece.

Multi-year support. Almost all participants deemed five years as the right length of time for the process. Some community foundations that grew the most and the fastest might have done as well with a three-year program. Some could have used more than five years to solidify gains made. But five years allowed each aspect of growth to develop to some extent in virtually all participating foundations.

"A good let-alone." It mattered greatly to participants that they were given "a good let-alone" — tremendous latitude in how they operated their development activities and their initiative. The project director subjected all questions of what was permissible within the Program's guidelines, as well as all requests for technical assistance, to only one litmus test: "Tell me how this will increase your capacity." All participants reported the value of this autonomy and support.

Managed support

Every element of the Program's "package of support" proved helpful to inducing rapid growth in the participating community foundations.

Annual meetings. Each January, the project director organized a separate meeting for each of the three Rounds. These meetings provided participants with an opportunity to share progress, discuss barriers, and learn from each other.

Executive directors, board chairs, and occasionally the key program officer were invited. Outside resource people also were brought in to conduct sessions when certain areas of expertise were requested, such as human resource management, communications strategies, inclusiveness, financial resource development, supervisory styles, and conflict resolution. The program evaluator was also called on to present "lessons learned so far" on a number of issues, and highlights from the year's survey of participants' growth data. Getting to know one's peers in other settings and learning from them was universally cited as a genuinely helpful feature of this Program.

Knowledge development and transfer. Another of Ford's goals for this Program was to increase the available body of knowledge on how community foundations grow to become increasingly capable institutions.

Ford made a grant to Rainbow Research, Inc. to conduct evaluation activities that would support this goal. This book is the culmination of that goal. A magazine, *CF/Findings from the Leadership Program for Community Foundations*, was produced annually for three years, which summarized the findings and observations about growth garnered from the year's visits to participating community foundations. Presented in a magazine-like format, the goal of the publication was to inform staffs and boards of other community foundations about the progress and lessons learned by Program participants.

While all community foundations in the country received free copies, the principal beneficiaries were those contemplating application to succeeding Rounds of the Program, some of whom became participants. Thus Round Two applicants benefited from the experience of Round One, and Round Three from the experience of both previous rounds. More broadly, non-participants had the opportunity to learn from the experience of participants.

Constructive site visit evaluations. Rainbow Research staff visited all Round One and Two participants in the first, second, and fifth year of their participation. During these visits, Rainbow Research staff conducted individual and group interviews with those who could shed light on the growing capacities of the foundation — staff, board, advisory groups, nonprofits and public partners, critics, and knowledgeable observers. These interviews asked groups to reflect on progress and momentary limits, their purpose, and their issues.

After each visit, Rainbow Research staff wrote a letter detailing observations to the executive director, with an official copy to the project director and the funder. These letters supported continued staff/board dialogue on capacity building.

Technical assistance. One important feature of the Program was a technical assistance fund, managed by the project director. The fund paid for skill development opportunities for both the foundation board and staff, including Council on Foundations conferences (especially by board members), staff development workshops, and meetings that directly related to their chosen program initiative (e.g., Children's Defense Fund meetings).

The technical assistance fund also supported the costs of consultants engaged by the community foundation to help with administrative issues, long-term resource development strategies, and marketing, and funded facilitators and speakers at board retreats or annual meetings. Yet even straightforward declarations from the project director that "you can use the technical assistance fund for anything that helps build your capacity," sometimes failed to engage participants' imaginations constructively. For example, some participants asked the fund to upgrade computer systems, while others struggled without such systems for years because they didn't think of the fund as a resource. Opinion was split on the advisability of giving guidelines or examples that illustrated the range of opportunities available versus requiring participants to think them up themselves.

Coaching on evaluation. A secondary goal of the Program was to increase participants' skills in evaluation. This was managed largely by demonstrating useful evaluation activities during site visits and partly by introducing principles of monitoring and self-evaluation through an annual survey of growth indicators. Results of these self-evaluations were presented at the annual meetings of participants and became the basis for strategy discussions.

Communications. The project director sent occasional memos to all participants, usually by Round. These highlighted upcoming events, new publications and materials, and news from individual participants. Most important, these communications underscored the collegial culture of the Program.

Special conferences. Participants in all three Rounds were offered the opportunity to participate in a special conference on program-related investments (PRIs). These conferences were supported by the Ford Foundation as part of a separate effort to build skills in the use of PRIs. At the request of Round Two executive directors, a special management clinic was convened for them. Round Two program directors also gathered in a special meeting on programming and grantmaking with support from the project director.

Encouragement for increased diversity. The Ford Foundation encouraged all participants, as it does all its grantees, to embrace the principles of its own adopted Pluralism Policy. This policy affirms the value of diversity, especially on boards of directors as well as among staff. Annual meetings of Program participants frequently featured discussions of the rewards and difficulties of implementing this policy, and annual surveys tracked the increasing percentage of minority and female members on the board, staff, and advisory committees. Ford carries on this interest through a program of support for 20 community foundations in its "Planning for Changing Communities, Diverse Needs" initiative.

Was it worth it?

In mid-1992, participants in all three Rounds were asked to list the benefits and the costs of the effort to play a stronger leadership role in the community. They were asked to enumerate "the ways in which the foundation has benefited, and the ways in which it has paid a price." They were then asked to compare the two lists and estimate the "net gain" on a scale of 1 to 5, with "1" meaning "paid dearly," "3 " meaning "gained and lost about equal," and "5" meaning "rewarded handsomely."

The "benefits" that were reported by more than half the participants were: increased visibility and enhanced reputation for the community foundation; increased funding for the issue area through the community foundation; and increased community foundation effectiveness. The only "cost" cited by more than half the participants: increased staff workload.

The average "net gain" across all three Rounds was 4.3, indicating the cost-benefit scale tipped heavily toward the "benefit" side. Furthermore, in Rounds One and Two, there were no ratings below a four, suggesting clear recognition of the benefits of a program such as this.

Interestingly, there is a slight trend over time: average ratings were highest for Round One (4.75), which had finished its five year stint in the Program, then for Round Two (4.5), which was midway through its fourth year, then for Round Three (3.67), which was midway through its second year. These differences suggest that (a) it takes some years to realize all the gains a program like this has to offer and/or (b) it's harder for the smallest community foundations, which Round Three participants were, to realize all the gains as fully as the largest ones. Both are probably true.

Implications for community groups wishing to build their own capacity

The results of the Leadership Program for Community Foundations are relevant not only to community foundations, but to a larger variety of community groups, as well. Any organization seeking to build capacity can benefit from the lessons learned by participants in the Program.

While written to address the challenges of community foundation growth, the categories and dynamics of capacity growth have application to the broader gamut of institutions presented in Chapter One, from families to local government to churches to development organizations. All these groups already have some measure of capacity, and all contribute to community capacity.

Look first to the four major areas for increased capacity outlined earlier in this chapter: organizational development, financial resource development, community leadership development, and grantmaking and programming practices. What community group would not become stronger if it found ways to develop its organizational capabilities, its resources, its role in the community, and its activities of gifting, service, and nurturance? What family would not become stronger, what government agency, what school or church?

Or re-organize these areas into the three ingredients of community capacity as discussed in Chapter One. "Commitment, resources, and skills" would seem critical to the healthy development of families, agencies, and other institutions. The ways in which they develop may vary but the necessity to develop these very ingredients of capacity, we believe, is the same. Furthermore, the conditions that allow and encourage these capacities to develop are clearly revealed in the design of the Leadership Program. The features of the Program that allowed community foundations to grow are very similar, we postulate, to the conditions that allow capacities to develop in the gamut of community institutions; they need only minor translation to fit the circumstances of families, for example, or school systems.

The community foundations studied in this project grew in their capacities because (a) they already had some capacity, and intended to develop it more, and (b) they were gifted and serviced by the growth-engendering features of the Leadership Program. Both parts helped, but not every group has the good fortune to be exposed to a growth program. Still, the lessons learned from this experience suggest that groups with some capacity (and we suggest all have some capacity) can, if they act intentionally, find and benefit from growth opportunities around them.

Here are some guidelines developed from clues gathered in this study. We believe they can be applied by all community groups

wishing to build capacity: They can be read from the perspective
of parent, neighbor, teacher, volunteer, advocate, executive, bu-
reaucrat, developer, and donor.

- *Focus on building your capacity.* Focus on building your
  ability to organize and share work among several people; on
  developing and holding financial resources and using a portion to grow further; on creating stronger links with other
  groups; and on helping other groups develop their capacities.

- *Focus on developing your commitment, resources, and skills.*
  Without them you have apathy, poverty, and ineptitude. Building capacity begins with marshaling in yourself and others the
  will to act; with attracting resources and developing ways to
  spend them wisely in pursuit of goals; and with forging partnerships with others that add or even multiply available
  strength.

- *Provide service to others, and get better at it.* Some portion of
  your commitment, resources, and skills is useful to others in
  helping them grow stronger; another portion is useful in helping your own group grow. The best activities do both.

- *Learn how the best do it.* There are lots of successful models
  to learn from, and it's a waste of scarce resources to imitate a
  third-rate program. Healthy growth, whether it's called quality
  of life, community viability, or organizational effectiveness, is
  built on good principles. Looking for good practice and successful activity of any kind is likely to be worth the effort.

- *Seek the collegial support of others.* Getting together with
  others doing similar work is an opportunity to swap insights,
  strategies, and support.

- *Seek assistance.* Whether it's called technical assistance,
  counseling, or friendship, there is no end to opportunities for
  getting help in efforts to grow and develop. While some ingredients of capacity may be easier to develop than others —

commitment versus resources, for example — there is every reason to think that the right assistance brings all key ingredients within closer reach.

- *Critique your progress.* Thinking about "the next level" of capacity, or what "making progress" is supposed to look like, helps you recognize whether you're getting there. Involving others in this reflection lets you get beyond the limitations of your own perspective.

Implications for institutions wishing to help community groups build their capacity

The clear success of this Program in helping community foundations reach new levels of capacity suggests that its design features can be replicated elsewhere by other programs intending to support a variety of community organizations and institutions. The following are recommendations to funders, programs and policy designers, organizational executives, business and community leaders, and government agencies wishing to help community groups build their capacity.

- *Make "capacity building" a legitimate goal for groups you support and keep the group's development central in making administrative decisions.* When a question comes up about what's permissible and what's not, use the litmus test, "How will this help you develop your own capacity, or that of another group you care about?"

- *Allow, through the design of the program, groups you support to work on two fronts simultaneously:* providing a service of some kind that benefits a segment of the community it cares about; AND developing their own commitment, resources, and skills in ways that can be sustained beyond the life of the grant.

• *Give groups you support the resources and encouragement to grow, not just the requirement.* Giving support is a gift indeed.

• *Bring groups you support together periodically to share insights, swap information, and strategize together.* Becoming part of a group (as distinct from staying isolated) helps significantly in building capacity.

• *Create a pool of funds that groups you support can tap to buy assistance from a provider of their choice.* This sends several important messages to grantees. "You're allowed to make mistakes, be in a quandary, experience a bit of failure or frustration, or otherwise not know exactly what to do. Help is available to you, and you're allowed and encouraged to use it without disgrace or penalty. You're encouraged to make choices of your own. We'll pay to help you grow." These messages allow a group to maintain dignity in the face of adversity.

• *Hold site visits where opinions are sought from a number of different stakeholders* (e.g., board members, advisors, intended beneficiaries, colleagues, and so on). Make them occasions to reflect on progress and barriers to progress, and to think creatively about options and priorities for the future.

• *Let the grantee develop its own program.* Community groups typically know, or can find out, what is opportune for their communities. A good capacity building grant is one that invests in the group's abilities to know or find out, rather than directing it to solutions or telling it what to do. This can be done without the funder giving up its own interests.

• *Help the group shop intelligently for resources.* Rather than tell it they need Consultant X or Training Group Y, help it frame the issue and what it wants a resource to do for/with it.

• *Keep paperwork to a minimum.* In a five-year program, annual reports to the funder proved to be sufficient. Ask a few broad questions about progress and expenditures. Let a telephone check-in by a project director or grants administration officer fill in the gaps. Further reporting should be supported by an evaluation line in the grantee's budget and be more about reflection and less about reporting.

- *Choose groups that have demonstrated through their record and their plans that they know how to grow.* Size isn't always a clue. Choose groups that can make the case that they can benefit substantially from the investment. Groups with the least record of growth may need more information on how to grow, and more support and encouragement. All groups have capacity to some degree, and all groups can increase their capacity given an opportunity tailored to their situation.

Implications for communities

The purposes of this book were threefold: to introduce the concept of community capacity; to show the role of community foundations as producers of community capacity; and to reveal the features of a program that successfully helped community foundations develop their capacity.

The experience of the Leadership Program points to these major lessons:

An organization's capacity can be increased. All participating organizations in the Program increased their capacity substantially, and worked to increase the capacity of other community groups they supported. "All it took" was a well-designed set of opportunities made available to a group of organizations with a demonstrated commitment to grow. The growth-inducing features of these opportunities have been discussed; we believe they can induce capacity growth elsewhere, whether imbedded in a formal

program or pieced together ad hoc. Community groups of all
kinds can find at least some of these features nearby or create
them for themselves. Funders and other leadership institutions
can incorporate these features into a myriad of other programs
if they wish to support the growing capacity of groups they care
about.

*Community groups can play constructive roles in the development
of another's capacity.* The community foundations in this Program
didn't grow in a vacuum. They grew because they became increasingly connected to the commitment, resources, and skills of others
around them — families, nonprofit groups, government agencies,
foundations, and others. The foundation grew from the exchange
and hopefully helped the others grow. We believe that other
kinds of community groups — groups that form the interlocking
puzzle design on the cover of this book — can become net contributors to a community's capacity. They can help solve problems
and seize opportunities when they both draw on the commitment,
resources, and skills of others, *and* help develop the commitment,
resources, and skills of others.

*Community foundations are especially well suited to be efficient
builders of community capacity.* Since community foundations relate to so many different kinds of community groups, they are in
an excellent position to draw from them and to give to them. Not
all community groups are as interconnected as community foundations. And none has the generic mission embraced by a growing
number of community foundations: to help the community address opportunities to improve its quality of life by cultivating the
philanthropy of individual and institutional donors and channeling
resources to do the greatest good.

Through the Leadership Program for Community Foundations,
participants have shown community foundations have the potential to play a pivotal role, leveraging commitment, resources, and
skills many times over in the service of community building.

Appendix A

Group of Advisors
Leadership Program for Community Foundations

Thomas Beech
Anne Burnett and Charles Tandy Foundation

William Diaz
Ford Foundation

Jean Fairfax
Arizona Community Foundation

Anne Farrell
The Seattle Foundation

Richard Green
Minneapolis Foundation

William Hart
Washington DC Community Foundation

Ira Hirschfield
Evelyn and Walter Haas Jr. Fund

Handy Lindsey
The Field Foundation

Continued

Leadership Program Group of Advisors, *continued*

Doug Jansson
Milwaukee Foundation

Alicia Philipp
Metropolitan Atlanta Community Foundation

R. Malcolm Salter
Hartford Foundation for Public Giving

Doris Sams
San Francisco Foundation

Lorie Slutsky
The New York Community Trust

Andrea Taylor
Ford Foundation

Appendix B

Directory of Participants
Leadership Program for Community Foundations

Round One (1987 - 1991)

Arizona Community Foundation
2122 East Highland Avenue, Suite 400
Phoenix, AZ 85016
    Stephen D. Mittenthal, President

Dade Community Foundation
200 South Biscayne Boulevard, Suite 4770
Miami, FL 33131
    Ruth Shack, President

The Dayton Foundation
2100 Kettering Tower
Dayton, OH 45423
    Frederick Bartenstein, III, Director (until September 1991)
    Darrell M. Murphy (1992 —)

El Paso Community Foundation
1616 Texas Commerce Bank Building
El Paso, TX 79901
    Janice W. Windle, President

Community Foundation of Greater Greenville
Post Office Box 6909
Greenville, SC 29606
    James B. Richmond, President (until July 1988)
    Jack Cromartie, President (early 1989 —)

Community Foundation of Greater Memphis
5210 Poplar Avenue, Suite 150
Memphis, TN 38119
> John K. Fockler, President (until mid-1989)
> Gid H. Smith, President (since mid-1989)

Rochester Area Foundation
335 East Main Street
Rochester, NY 14604
> Linda S. Weinstein, President (until 1993)
> Jennifer Leonard, President (1993 —)

Community Foundation for Southeastern Michigan
333 West Fort Street, Suite 2010
Detroit, MI 48226
> Mariam C. Noland, President

Round Two (1989 - 1993)

Baltimore Community Foundation
2 East Read Street, Ninth Floor
Baltimore, MD 21202
> Eugene Struckhoff, President (until 1990)
> Timothy Armbruster, President (1990 —)

The Community Foundation for Greater Lorain County
1865 North Ridge Road, Suite A
Lorain, OH 44055
> Carol G. Simonetti, Executive Director

Madison Community Foundation
615 East Washington Avenue
Madison, WI 53701
> Jane T. Coleman, Executive Director

Greater New Orleans Foundation
2515 Canal Street, Suite 401
New Orleans, LA 70119
> Patricia C. Mason, Executive Director (until 1992)
> Gregory Ben Johnson, Executive Director (1992 —)

Central New York Community Foundation
500 South Salina Street, Suite 428
Syracuse, NY 13202
  Margaret G. Ogden, President

✓ Foundation Northwest
400 Paulsen Center, Suite 400
421 West Riverside
Spokane, WA 99201
  Jeanne L. Ager, Executive Director (until mid 1990)
  Peter A. Jackson, President (1991 —)

The Community Foundation Serving Richmond and Central Virginia
9211 Forest Hill Avenue, Suite 109
Richmond, VA 23235
  Darcy S. Oman, President

East Tennessee Foundation
360 Sovran Center
550 W. Main Avenue
Knoxville, TN
  Katharine K. Pearson, Executive Director

Greater Triangle Community Foundation
Post Office Box 12834
100 Park Drive, Suite 209
Research Triangle Park, NC 27709
  Shannon E. St. John, Executive Director

Tucson Community Foundation
8842 East Tanque Verde, Suite D
Tucson, AZ 85715
  Donna L. Grant, Executive Director

Round Three (1991 - 1995)

Delaware Community Foundation
Post Office Box 25207
Wilmington, DE 19899
  Collis O. Townsend, Executive Director

Duluth-Superior Area Community Foundation
227 West First Street, Suite 618
Duluth, MN 55802
   Holly C. Sampson, President

Fargo-Moorhead Area Foundation
15 Broadway, Suite 601
Fargo, ND 58102
   Susan M. Hunke, Executive Director

The Community Foundation of Greater Greensboro
Post Office Box 207
Greensboro, NC 27402
   Wentworth Durgin, Executive Director

Maine Community Foundation
Post Office Box 148
210 Main Street
Ellsworth, ME 04605
   Marian M. Kane, President

Rockford Community Trust
333 East State Street
Post Office Box 111
Rockford, IL 61104
   Gloria Lundin, Executive Director

Sacramento Regional Foundation
1610 Arden Way, Suite 298
Sacramento, CA 95815
   David F. Hess, Executive Director

Community Foundation of Greater Santa Cruz County
820 Bay Avenue, Suite 210
Capitola, CA 95010
   Grace Jepsen, Executive Director

Vermont Community Foundation
Post Office Box 30
2 Court Street
Middlebury, VT 05753
   David G. Rahr, Executive Director

References

Brown, Prudence. Personal communication, 1993

Bothwell, Robert O. "Are They Worthy of the Name?: A Critic's View." In Magat, *An Agile Servant: Community Leadership by Community Foundations.* Produced by The National Agenda for Community Foundations' Community Leadership Project of the Council on Foundations. NY: The Foundation Center, 1989.

Columbus Foundation Annual Survey, 1992

Council on Foundations, "Community Foundations at 75: A Report on the Status of Community Foundations," Washington, DC: Council on Foundations, 1989

Council on Foundations. "1991 Survey of Community Foundations: Preliminary Results," Washington DC: Council on Foundations, 1991

Council on Foundations, "Definition of a U.S. Community Foundation." Washington, DC: Council on Foundations, 1992(a)

Continued

Council on Foundations. "Community Foundations in 1990: A Report on the Status of Community Foundations," Washington, DC: Council on Foundations, 1992(b)

Ford Foundation. "Status Report on the Community Foundation Initiative," A confidential report for discussion at the June 1986 Trustees' meeting

Foundation Center. *Foundation Giving: Yearbook of Facts and Figures on Private, Corporate and Community Foundations, 1991 Edition.* NY: Foundation Center, 1991

Foundation Center. *The Foundation Directory, 1992 Edition.* NY: The Foundation Center, 1992

Gardner, John W. *Building Community.* Washington, DC: Independent Sector, 1991

Hammack, David C. "Community Foundations: The Delicate Question of Purpose," In Magat, Richard (Ed.), *An Agile Servant: Community Leadership by Community Foundations.* NY: The Foundation Center, 1989.

Joseph, James A. *The Charitable Impulse.* NY: The Foundation Center, 1989(a).

Joseph, James A. "Leadership in Community Foundations," In Magat, Richard (Ed.), *An Agile Servant: Community Leadership by Community Foundations.* NY: The Foundation Center, 1989(b).

Joseph, James A., from his 1989 address to the El Paso Community Foundation, cited in "El Paso Community Foundation," Fall 1990, Vol 1, Number 1.

Kretzmann, John P. and John L. McKnight, 1993. **Building Communities From the Inside Out: A Path Toward Finding and Mobilizing a Community's Assets.** Evanston, IL: Center for Urban Affairs and Policy Research, Northwestern University, 1993

Leonard, Jennifer. "Creating Community Capital: Birth and Growth of Community Foundations." In Magat, Richard (Ed.), **An Agile Servant: Community Leadership by Community Foundations.** NY: The Foundation Center, 1989.

Magat, Richard (Ed.). **An Agile Servant: Community Leadership by Community Foundations.** Produced by The National Agenda for Community Foundations' Community Leadership Project of the Council on Foundations. NY: The Foundation Center, 1989.

Magat, Richard. "Agility, Leadership, Myth, and Reality: An Introduction." In Magat, Richard (Ed.), **An Agile Servant: Community Leadership by Community Foundations.** NY: The Foundation Center, 1989.

Mayer, Steven E. "Growth Factors in the Development of Community Foundations: A Study Guide for Technical Assistance," Minneapolis: Rainbow Research, Inc., 1988

National Committee for Responsive Philanthropy, "Responsive Philanthropy," Summer 1991.

Newman, Bruce L. "Pioneers of the Community Foundation Movement." In Magat, Richard (Ed.), **An Agile Servant: Community Leadership by Community Foundations.** NY: The Foundation Center, 1989.

Peirce, Neal. In plenary session, Fall Conference for Community Foundations, Puerto Rico, 1992

Continued

Rainbow Research, Inc., "CF/Findings from the Leadership Program for Community Foundations," Growth Series and Leadership Series. Minneapolis: Rainbow Research, Inc., 1989, 1990, 1991

The Stevens Group, "Growing Up Nonprofit: An Essay on Nonprofit Life Cycle Development." Minneapolis: The Stevens Group, 1993.

Struckhoff, Eugene C. *Ways To Grow: A Study of Community Foundations Serving Populations Under 250,000* Washington, DC: Council on Foundations, 1991

Ylvisaker, Paul N. "Community and Community Foundations in the Next Century." In Magat, Richard (Ed.), *An Agile Servant: Community Leadership by Community Foundations.* NY: The Foundation Center, 1989.